KATIE TAYLOR

KATIE TAYLOR

AND JOHNNY WATTERSON

My Olympic Dream

**SIMON &
SCHUSTER**

London · New York · Sydney · Toronto · New Delhi

A CBS COMPANY

First published in Great Britain by Simon & Schuster UK Ltd, 2012
A CBS Company

1 3 5 7 9 10 8 6 4 2

Simon & Schuster UK Ltd
1st Floor
222 Gray's Inn Road
London WC1X 8HB

www.simonandschuster.co.uk

Simon & Schuster Australia,
Sydney

Simon & Schuster India,
New Delhi

A CIP catalogue record for this book is
available from the British Library

ISBN 978-1-47112-593-5

Designed by Jacqui Caulton

Printed and bound in Great Britain by
Butler Tanner and Dennis, Frome, Somerset

CONTENTS

For His Honour
God honours those who honour Him.

'For I know the plans I have for you,' declares the Lord,
'plans to prosper you and not to harm you, plans to give
you hope and a future.'

Jeremiah 29:11

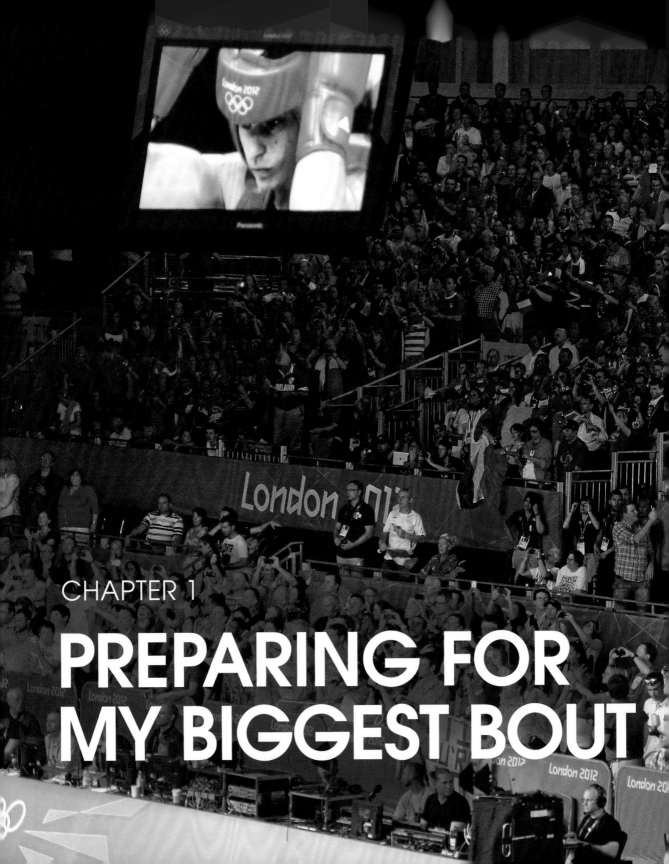

CHAPTER 1

PREPARING FOR MY BIGGEST BOUT

He trains my hands for battle.

My Olympic Dream

Rituals are important.

As far back as I can remember, I dreamed of becoming an Olympic champion and I imagined standing on the podium and having the gold medal placed around my neck. Most kids have big dreams like that, every child wants to be a professional footballer or a great champion or a movie star but for most people, life has a way of telling you that you're wasting your time with fanciful dreams. I guess I never got that memo! As I got older and became more involved with sport, my child-like dreams became my desires and my desires became my ambitions, until winning an Olympic gold medal became the most important personal goal of my life. I didn't even know what my sport would be at that time, I just knew there was an Olympic champion in my heart.

Mam was with me on the morning of the Olympic final against Sofya Ochigava. She had come over to my apartment in the athletes' village in Stratford in the east end of London to help me prepare for the bout. In a few hours' time I would fight against the Russian for the gold medal, and after that my Olympics would be over.

After nearly 150 fights and four world championship gold medals, she doesn't need to ask me what I want her to do, our preparation

(Previous page)
Preparing to fulfil my
Olympic dream.

is the same every time. She picked up my hairbrush, wet my hair as she always does, and began to put it into plaits. I was standing with my back to her and, as she was doing my hair, she prayed out loud over me. I could sense the emotion in her voice but she had to hold it together for my sake, this is perhaps the most important part of my pre-fight ritual. Ma repeated some of Psalm 18 to me, which is one of my favourite pieces from the scriptures. This is a psalm that I regularly read when I am away in competition. It is a reminder that it is God that trains my mind for battle and He is my shield of victory.

The focus of our prayers was to ask that I performed to the best of my ability and that I was able to express that ability when I stepped into the ring later. It was also about praying that God would help me deal with any negativity that might creep into my mind, or any comments from outside that might distract me. I tried to listen to what He was saying about me and not what other people were saying. It was important for me to be reminded that my Olympic dream began first in the heart of God before it ever began in me – this was my God-given destiny!

The night before, Mam had spent some time praying about what scripture she was going to read to me. It's never a random choice of words plucked from the pages of the Bible. She wants the meaning to be specific to the moment and to my needs, something that she could share with me that would give me assurance and confidence.

With my mam, Bridget, at Dublin airport.

My mam carries the
Olympic flame at Ely Place,
Dublin, on 6 June 2012
as part of the Olympic
torch relay.

Mam is my spiritual rock and she is as much a part of my boxing team as anyone else, but she also has a great understanding of the sport. It may surprise you to learn that she was the first in our family to challenge the view that women and boxing don't mix, for in the late 1980s she became the first female judge to be appointed in Ireland. Needless to say, she faced a lot of opposition at that time from within the boxing community but now it is commonplace to see female judges and referees. I like to think that I have carried on her pioneering spirit.

Sofya Ochigava

For my final against Sofya Ochigava, Mam picked a scripture from the book of Isaiah that speaks about what God said about people with faith: 'That no weapon formed against you will prevail and that you will refute every tongue that accuses you and that this is the heritage of those that belong to the Lord.'

That might seem like a strange choice of scripture from all of the promises of the Bible, but it was exactly what I needed to hear, because my Russian opponent had been publicly saying some bad things about me in the days leading up to the final. I didn't know at the time exactly what she had said, but I knew she had been disrespectful.

These verses reminded me that Ochigava's critical words were just dirty tactics in an attempt to undermine my confidence in my Olympic dream. The words were a promise that God will shield me from any negativity and accusations that are thrown in my direction. If I had spent any energy before the fight dwelling on Ochigava's comments, then her tactics would have worked. But the verses my mam gave me were telling me not to focus on who was standing opposite me in the ring, but to focus on the God who is always standing beside me, both in and out of the ring.

For those who think that I saw the fight as an opportunity to settle a score with Ochigava, I can honestly say that her words were not a motivating factor at all. Ochigava had said a lot of disrespectful things, but at the time I didn't fully realise the extent of what it was, as I had avoided the newspapers and was too focused on my own build-up to worry about anything else that might have been going on.

'That no weapon formed against you will prevail and that you will refute every tongue that accuses you and that this is the heritage of those that belong to the Lord.'

I had heard that negative words had been said only because a journalist came up to me after one of the earlier fights in the ExCeL Arena and mentioned it. Although it was in most of the newspapers and online, even now I don't fully know all the details. To be honest I was surprised with her, that sort of behaviour is usually more common in professional boxing than in the amateur code.

I'm hardly a stranger to criticism and I had faced these kinds of battles many times throughout my career. From the beginning when I was starting out, I had to fight for the right just to be allowed to climb through the ropes as a woman and box. In those days, female boxing wasn't sanctioned by the boxing association, but my dad would tuck my hair up into my headgear and let me box against the boys. When asked what my name was, he would just say K.Taylor, as giving my full name would have obviously given the game away. More recently, for women's boxing to earn acceptance into the Olympic Games was a struggle. All the way through my career, there has always been negativity about what I (and others like me) am doing. So having to deal with some pre-fight name-calling wasn't about to distract me.

What little I knew of what she had said sounded absurd, but I had wrapped myself in my own bubble and wasn't thinking about anything outside the bubble except the fight. All day before my bout, I had my phone turned off and deliberately blocked myself off from

Adriano Araujo (in red) of Brazil in action against Sofya Ochigava in the Olympic semi-final.

the outside world. Ochigava's mind games didn't even register with me. If they had any effect at all, it was probably to reinforce the support I was given in the ExCeL Arena.

Over the last couple of years when we've boxed each other in big championships at European or world level, our rivalry has sharpened. Outside the ring, we say hello, we're not unfriendly, but that's about it. Years ago, when we were in different weight classes, we'd probably have gone out after the competition, sat around and had a coffee. We were friendly and I found her quite a funny person to be with. But now we are in the same weight division, that option has gone – it's difficult to be close to girls you are competing against on a regular basis. Regardless of what she said, I still think she's a nice girl and her comments were uncharacteristic. She is a very talented boxer who is great for the sport.

Dad has since said to me that he thought she might be getting her excuses in first, and that maybe it was also the pressure of the occasion building up within her that made her say these things. She wasn't the only one: I felt under pressure too. But how could I not feel it, given my own ambition to win the gold medal?

Ochigava celebrates her victory against Araujo that set up her bout against me.

Under Pressure

All pressure is relative, but I'd be lying if I said I didn't feel it bearing down heavily on me. In every contest I've ever fought, there is some pressure to deal with. Often the greatest pressure is that which I put on myself. I knew the fans expected me to do well, and by now

> Being a champion means that I live permanently with the need to keep winning to maintain that status – and I could accept that.

I was very aware of the massive support for me around London and back home in Ireland. So this time, I was feeling the pressure of other people's expectations creeping into my head in a way that I hadn't experienced to the same degree before. Normally, I'm strong at keeping out external things, but this Olympic final was something I had never faced before.

What's more, I could look on the positive side of the pressure of expectation. If I hadn't won the World Championship, there wouldn't have been as much focus on me. Being a champion means that I live permanently with the need to keep winning to maintain that status – and I could accept that. That's how it has been since the start of my career and it wasn't going to change now, especially not now.

However much I tried to downplay the pressure, I was almost fighting with myself during the build-up as doubts crept in. I suffered what I can only describe as unsettling waves of nerves. It wasn't the waiting that caused it. Other boxers have said to me in the past that it's the hanging around to get into the ring that really kills them, but I normally enjoy that part. I like the process and the anticipation.

This time, however, I wanted it to be over and done with, and that was a terrible way to think. On a couple of occasions in previous fights, when I haven't been able to enjoy the process of the build-up, I've fought and lost. I found it unnerving that on the most important day of my boxing life, and on the verge of fulfilling the dreams I've carried in my heart since I was a young girl, the nerves were knotting in my stomach and a part of me didn't want to face the battle.

Struggling to cope with finals is not what people expect of me. I think they believe that because I have won so many titles at European and world level, I'm mentally capable of coping with any boxing situation, and usually I am. It's one of the strongest facets of my game.

But, like anyone, I can have doubts, and it's at these times when it is so important to remind myself of the promises of God for my life. I remember speaking a verse from the book of Philippians to myself, it says: 'I can do all things through Christ who gives me strength.'

Family Support

In their support for me, my family play different roles, Mam prays and Dad talks tactics. On the morning of the final, Dad came over to me in the Olympic Village. We wanted to make sure that Thursday 9 August 2012 was no different from over a dozen important finals I've been in, and we went for a walk as we always do. We walked for about 30 minutes, and it didn't matter where we went. We talked about the fight, how it was going to go, what might or might not happen, and how I was feeling – anything that we thought needed to be aired. This time was also about relaxing, getting prepared and being with someone I trusted, somewhere other than sat in my room.

Whatever city we are in, we have always found a route and we do the same walk over and over throughout the week. It's part of an unbreakable routine we have on competition day, and that day it began early at 8.00am when I had to get up for the weigh-in. After the scales, I went back to my room for breakfast instead of going to the main dining hall, because I wanted privacy and some space to do my own thing.

It was about 11 when Dad called so we could go for our walk, and we strolled out from the village up to Olympic Park and around by the athletics stadium, a vast, wide area where you can look across and see the velodrome, the aquatic centre and the basketball arena. When we came back, Mam arrived at about two o'clock to do my hair and pray. It's the same ritual all the time and it has worked for me for years. It's a case of 'if it's not broke don't fix it'. We never change.

Throughout the day, I listen to the same worship songs on my iPod and I read the same Bible verses. When I'm boxing or preparing for a fight, it's when I feel closest to God. This Olympic dream was too big for me to deal with on my own, so for the last ten years, I have relied on God and I've put everything in His hands. It's hard to put everything you hold dear in the hands of someone else, because it's natural to want to be in control, but I've learned from experience that God will never let me down so I just try to trust Him.

The journey to the ExCeL centre from the village was about 30 minutes by bus. The team with me consisted of my dad, Irish head coach Billy Walsh and Zauri Antia, Ireland's technical coach. There were very few words spoken, except by Billy and Zauri, who were cracking a few jokes to try to lighten the mood. Once inside the arena, I stuck to the same routine and did the same warm-up in the changing room as I'd done for my previous fights. I have quite a long warm-up session, which lasts maybe 45 or 50 minutes. I always wear the same warm-up tee-shirt which said on the front 'It is God who arms me with strength' and on the back were the words 'He trains my hands for battle'.

Before we left the tunnel for the final, my dad was constantly giving me instructions, reinforcing what he has been saying to me in the warm-up area. He kept on repeating what he wanted me to do for the first 30 seconds of the first round, going over the tactics he had planned for the fight.

His message to me was: 'Keep using your left hand. Don't stay still – feint. Keep jabbing. Use your left hand. Be patient.' That's all he said. It was the same repetition to try to put simple stuff in my head. He kept repeating, repeating, repeating. After almost 150 fights, I know now how we do it, but I know Dad was feeling under huge pressure too, because when I'm in the ring, the relationship is not just coach and boxer, it's also father and daughter. That makes it twice the pressure.

The Warm-up

I used my long warm-up to focus on the fight and after that I practiced some combinations and some shadow boxing specific to how I was going to try to fight against Ochigava. After the pads, I walked around stretching, trying to see things in my head. Dad was focused and so was I. Some people can joke and laugh minutes before a fight, but Dad and me are the opposite and are really intense people to be around during that time. He became so nervous I could see the colour of his face draining away.

In training with Dad, wearing my favourite tee-shirt.

It didn't help that from where we were in the locker room, we could hear everything that was going on outside in the boxing arena. The music was blaring and the crowd cheered and clapped every time they announced a celebrity in the arena. Before I went out for my final, I didn't know exactly who was in the crowd, but I was told afterwards that former heavyweight champion Evander Holyfield had attended, and so did the British prime minister David Cameron and Olympic silver medallist Amir Khan.

I could hear the interview former world champion Barry McGuigan gave before my fight. Every introduction and announcement was audible, as the changing area was right beside the crowd. Ideally I like a quiet area to warm up in, but for an Olympic final you cannot expect to have such a luxury. Although I have no doubt it all added to the atmosphere, the last thing I wanted in my ear were the celebrity announcements coming in from the public address system; all I wanted to do was concentrate on the fight ahead. Much as I tried to shut myself off and detach myself, there was nothing I could do about it. In these situations when you can't control things, you just have to get on with it.

As I waited, I could sense the whole place was on edge; the atmosphere was so lively, more like a carnival or a concert than an amateur fight. I got my first direct taste of this when I walked out with Billy Walsh under the stands to have the bandages on my hands stamped by officials. The area where this was done was right out on the concourse of the arena, and when the crowd saw me at the official's table, everyone began screaming my name: 'Katie! Katie! Katie!' I realised then how many of the fans were Irish. It was crazy and on a completely different scale to anything I'd experienced at European or World Championship finals. When Billy Walsh came back into the warm-up area with me, he commented to my dad that the hairs on the back of his neck were standing up as the atmosphere was electric. There were tri-colours everywhere, a sea of green, white and orange.

Irish fans flood into the ExCeL Arena – the support I received was unbelievable.

Beating Caroline Barry in the O2 in Dublin in 2009 – a bout that gave me a taste of what it was like to box in front of a big crowd.

The nearest I'd ever experienced to anything like this was the time I'd fought on the undercard of Bernard Dunne in his world title fight against Ricardo Cordoba in March 2009 at the Dublin O2. Dad had been approached by boxing promoter Brian Peters, who managed Dunne, about the possibility of me boxing on the show. Even though at that time I was twice world champion and three times European champion, I had rarely boxed in Ireland. This contest was going to be shown live on national TV, so it was a great opportunity for me to box in front of the Irish public. I had been as a spectator to a few of Brian Peters' shows, so I knew it would be professionally run and it would be a full house. I couldn't turn down the opportunity to box in front of a capacity home crowd.

My fight that night, against the American Caroline Barry, had been a dress rehearsal for this Olympic final. Even then, Dad was thinking ahead to the Olympics. He knew then that the ExCeL held 10,000 people and that it would be full. So he wanted me to experience boxing in front of that sort of crowd before I got to the Olympics, as the crowds we usually box in front of are much smaller, usually no more than 200 people, though I had fought in front of a much larger crowd when I beat Cheng Dong in China for my second world title. Being on the undercard at Bernard's fight meant I had experienced a walk to the ring like this before, with thousands of people screaming. Brian had organised a big entrance for my fight: a U2 song was blasting out and he had mock heads of U2 jumping around me as I walked to the ring. This was a different ball game altogether.

Dad saw the benefits back then when nobody else could, and he had to push hard for me to be included in the show, despite some opposition from the Irish Boxing Association. They didn't like the idea of an amateur boxer appearing on the same card as professional boxers when a world title was up for grabs. Admittedly, it is unusual for pros and amateurs to box on the same bill. Getting the go-ahead to box was just another couple of rounds Dad had to go through on my behalf.

Thanks to the preparation I'd done, the previous successes I'd had in the ring and the support I had around me, it seemed the stage was set for me to take the gold medal, but the battle was still raging in my mind. This Olympic final would challenge all of my convictions. It was a game within a game. I was bursting to go, but I had to stay calm.

> It was a game within a game. I was bursting to go, but I had to stay calm. I had worked for it for my whole life, but had to think in small steps through eight minutes.

Entering the arena ahead of my Olympic title fight. Zauri Antia is on the left and Dad on the right. You can see the tension in our faces.

I had worked for it for my whole life, but had to think in small steps through eight minutes. I was blessed to be here, but to be here was never going to be enough; I had to win. How many world champions are beaten in their first fights? Despite the best-laid plans of so many great athletes over the years, the Olympic Games have a habit of writing their own stories.

Those were the thoughts creeping into my head as I got ready to fight – strangely baffling doubts. I didn't want to fall at the final hurdle, and I was hoping this wasn't going to be one of those sorry tales. I didn't want this night, of all nights, to be my career flaw. Five European Championships, four World Championships and the Olympic silver medal would have been no more than a lost gold to me. It was that simple. So I did what I always do, I turned to the Bible. I was about to walk into the arena and I was reciting Psalm 37 to myself: 'Delight yourself in the Lord and He will give you the desires of your heart.'

I was blessed to be here, but to be here was never going to be enough; I had to win. How many world champions are beaten in their first fights?

That's the mental battle I faced before going into the arena, and those verses cleared my head. Just as it had felt when I walked around the Olympic Stadium during the opening ceremony, I realised it was just another step closer to the goal I had set for myself. Carrying the flag that night was the start of the last lap of a journey that had begun when I was ten; now I was in the final home straight.

Into the Ring

I had my mouthguard already in place before we left the locker room, which is something Dad and Zauri laugh at me about. When they put the gumshield in, they say it turns a switch inside my head and my face completely changes. So they put it in before I walked to the ring. The switch was tripped as the three of us stepped from the tunnel for my final walk to the Olympic ring. Everything else was blanked out.

I expected the crowd's reaction and I knew there was going to be a rush of noise. There was and it was a wild, bring-the-roof-down welcome, but I couldn't allow myself to enjoy it. It was tempting to take a quick glance up and say: 'Wow! How great is this!' But I couldn't break my focus like that. I felt energised by the noise. I felt my nerves

Dad checks my headgear before the fight begins.

and the expectation on me, but I was also confident that if I performed to my ability that I could win. Dad was just telling me to relax and stay focused. So there was no other thought in my head except winning as I walked towards the ring.

I never looked up to the crowd. I didn't allow myself become drained or distracted. Other boxers I know glance around and suck up the energy and feed off it, or they smile and wave at everybody, or jump up on the ropes and shake their fists in delight to pump themselves up. That impulse was hanging there, but I ignored it. I ducked under the ropes and was so focused that I really couldn't hear much at all. The only voice I could distinguish was Dad's, which I've learned over the years to pick out. Everything else coming from around the ring was muddled, background noise.

I was entering the ring for my Olympic final, and there was no place in the world I would rather have been. I believed the moment was mine and this was my destiny. It was going to be hard, very hard; I knew I needed to maintain my discipline and make no mistakes. But if I did all of that, I believed I could win. I'd beaten her 11-7 earlier in 2012 to win the World Championship in China, and defeated her 10-5 the previous year to take the European Championship. None of that mattered now; this was a clean slate. The more you box against the same opponent the harder it becomes, you both become familiar with each other.

I walked to the centre of the ring towards Ochigava's corner. I touched her glove with mine. I listened to the referee speaking. I thanked God for what He had already given me. I heard the bell and we began to box.

As expected, the first 30 seconds were tense, neither of us willing to show our hand first. I tried to let a combination off but I felt like there was a weight on my shoulders – I didn't know if it was the pressure. During that period, I couldn't put my shots together. I could see all the punches coming at me, but I couldn't react to them normally. I was stepping back out of the way, and though I wasn't getting hit, I was unable to come back with my usual combinations. It was the first time this had ever happened. I couldn't let it worry me, but I had to work out a response – and quickly.

I was in an Olympic final and I was thinking to myself: 'What am I going to do?' This is when prayer matters. After about 30 seconds, the weight lifted and my punches started to flow, but I knew I had one tough fight on my hands . . .

> I was entering the ring for my Olympic final, and there was no place in the world I would rather have been.

CHAPTER 2

EARLY DAYS

You can lead by example.

Childhood Games

Oldcourt, a council estate in the south-west end of the seaside town of Bray, is my home. It is where I was raised and where I still live. It is also where I first fell in love with sport.

I was definitely a tomboy growing up. You could always find my brother Peter and I out on the streets kicking a ball around with the lads in the area. We played on a patch of green directly in front of our house, which is known to everyone in the estate as 'the bank'. There weren't any real facilities there, but we needed only a ball and a couple of jumpers for goals. We would play for hours, sometimes until it got dark and we could no longer see the football.

Peter and I hung around together all the time back then, so much so that people thought we were twins, even though he was more than a year older than me. We were, and still are, very close. I trailed around after him almost everywhere. Like me, Peter loved his sport. During my earlier boxing years, when he was competing himself, we would train together almost every night. Over the years, I have learned lots from him, in both boxing and football, without even thinking. If he did it, I copied. I wanted to do everything like he did.

As a child, I can hardly remember a day where I wasn't playing some sort of sport. To some that might not sound like much of a

(*Previous page*)
Lining up for Ireland.

childhood, but I loved it – sport was all that ever captured my interest. So I joined as many of the local clubs as was physically possible: I played Gaelic football and camogie for Bray Emmets and Fergal Ógs, ran with Bray Runners, played soccer with St Fergal's FC and after that for Newtown Juniors and I boxed with Bray Boxing Club. On top of that, I would play for my school, and for county and sometimes even international teams. There were days where I'd play a Gaelic match for my school, then a football match in the early evening, which would finish just in time for me to catch the end of a training session in the boxing club. On the day of my first-ever boxing exhibition, I came straight to my fight after winning an athletics cross-country race only an hour previously. I don't know where I got the energy from!

By the time I was about ten years old, my dad would train me and the other junior boxers for an hour from six to seven, and then he would train the men from eight onwards. But he would let Peter and I stay on and train with the men, too. I was so competitive that I'd be thinking to myself: 'Next week, I'm going to be better than all of the other kids because I'm training more than they are!' That was just how I was wired: focused and determined even then, always trying to be the best I could be.

I wasn't just that intense with boxing either. Whether I was playing a football match or running in the school races, it was never a game or a pastime to me. Not that I didn't enjoy it – I loved it and I couldn't have imagined spending my time doing anything else, but I was just never able to take

Dressed up smart for a formal photo at St Fergal's National School.

As a young girl I took part in as many sports as I could. Here I am at a Bray Running Club event.

a light-hearted approach. When the other kids were running around laughing and playing and enjoying the occasion, I would be off by myself trying to focus on what I needed to do to win. My mam worried about me being so competitive at that age. When she looked at how I approached events, compared to other kids my age, she was concerned that I wasn't enjoying it. But that was me. I enjoyed the events, but I enjoyed them so much more when I won!

It seemed that even at a young age, I was destined to break down barriers in how people perceive women in sport. I had always played with and against the boys without ever thinking it was unusual. Most of the lads on the local teams had grown up playing against me, so they didn't think anything of it either. I would only ever get a reaction when my team played against sides from other counties, where the players or their parents had never seen a girl play football before, and certainly not with the boys.

The odd time, you could hear them snigger and joke before the match. Then I'd hit them with the first hard tackle and they would soon forget I was a girl! I still get this reaction sometimes when I go to training camps with the lads. I'll be paired up to spar with one of the men from one of the other national teams, and he would be standing across the ring from me joking with his team-mates, who have stopped training to watch him humiliate the girl from Ireland who had the cheek to show up at a men's training camp. But when the spar starts, it's usually not long before the joking stops. It's not that I go to these training camps with an agenda, I'm genuinely not trying to prove anything, I just want to be treated like any other boxer there.

At the time when I was playing with Newtown Juniors, one of the local football teams that played in the Wicklow League, girls were allowed to play up until they were 12 years old, but then they had to join an all-girls team. But the year I became too old for the Under-12 team, I was chosen as the Wicklow School'boy' Player of the Year and was selected for the county team to play in the national inter-county tournament, called the Kennedy Cup.

I had always played with and against the boys without ever thinking it was unusual.

Wicklow's Kennedy Cup team. I was thrilled to play in the national tournament.

Lining up for Newtown Juniors – the local league changed its rules so I could continue to play with the boys.

It was the first time a girl had received the league's Player of the Year award and also the first time a girl had been selected for the county team. Because I proved that I was up to the same standard as the schoolboy players, the Wicklow League made every effort to accommodate me, changing the age limit for girls to play on boys' teams to Under-14, so I was able to play for an extra two years with the lads. I was thrilled because there weren't a lot of girls' teams around and I wanted to play at the highest possible standard.

Competing with the lads had probably begun in our kitchen with my brothers, but that trend continued right the way up through my sporting history. I believe that having the opportunity to do so has greatly helped my athletic ability, particularly in boxing. It was very important in my development, especially in later years when I started to box and play football at international level.

Starting to Box

I trained with the boys from the first time I stepped into a boxing gym and now I still spar with international-standard male boxers when I'm preparing for any of my major competitions. My opinion would be that every female athlete should train with men if they can. There are obvious advantages to training with people who are naturally stronger than you.

When I first started boxing, there wasn't a boxing club in Bray, but my dad was training in a club in a nearby village called Enniskerry, and he would take me and my brothers along with him. The building itself was an old, damp hall with cigarette butts on the floor from the bingo the night before. Because of the age restrictions in amateur boxing, that was also my dad's last year of competitive fighting, so he decided to turn his hand to coaching and he started his own club in Bray.

My opinion would be that every female athlete should train with men if they can.

We rented a large corrugated iron hut across the road from our estate, which was known to everyone as the 'Tin Can'. It was basic but we loved it; it was our first real boxing home. There were two columns of bags running down either side, and a stage at one end where we'd put up a makeshift ring. After a couple of years in the Tin Can we were on the move again – the building was getting knocked down and redeveloped – so we moved to a balcony in a local sports hall to continue our training.

An early shot of me, aged ten, training in Bray.

I knew what positions I had to take up during the matches, but I didn't have that type of fitness or the stamina in my legs to get there.

The frustration wasn't the only issue in the end, more critically it stopped being enjoyable. I would still give it everything I had and tried to be as physical as I could, tried to look for the ball all of the time and I always pushed to get my tackles in. I knew what positions I had to take up during the matches, but I didn't have that type of fitness or the stamina in my legs to get there. Boxing is a completely different type of fitness from football. In boxing, I compete over four two-minute rounds. A football match is 90 minutes and demands a different set of muscles and stamina.

I was also beginning to arrive late into challenges. I realised that the less frequently I played, the more my timing was off. Not only was I almost injuring myself with some late, mistimed challenges, but on one occasion during a big European qualifier against Italy, I managed to get myself sent off.

Looking back now, I can see the funny side. I had received a yellow card after a late challenge in the first half, but minutes earlier had actually scored a cracking goal putting us 1-0 up at the break. I remember Noel King saying to me at half time: 'Be careful not to get sent off in the second half.' He explained that we couldn't afford to end the game with only ten players on the pitch. Five minutes into the second half, I went in for a challenge, mistimed it again and I got sent off. Noel was understanding about it. After all, he couldn't say a lot as I think he was sent off a few and he would take me and my brothers along with him. The building itself was an old, damp hall with cigarette butts on the floor from the bingo the night before. Because of the age restrictions in amateur boxing, that was also

My opinion would be that every female athlete should train with men if they can.

my dad's last year of competitive fighting, so he decided to turn his hand to coaching and he started his own club in Bray.

We rented a large corrugated iron hut across the road from our estate, which was known to everyone as the 'Tin Can'. It was basic but we loved it; it was our first real boxing home. There were two columns of bags running down either side, and a stage at one end where we'd put up a makeshift ring. After a couple of years in the Tin Can we were on the move again – the building was getting knocked down and redeveloped – so we moved to a balcony in a local sports hall to continue our training.

An early shot of me, aged ten, training in Bray.

Sparring with Michael
O'Brien in the Tin Can.

It never really met our needs, as the floor was concrete, which wasn't good for the joints, there was nowhere to hang a bag, and putting a ring up was like trying to set up scaffolding before every session. We moved around like nomads for a few years, from building to building, from hall to hall. We even had a stint training out of a classroom in a local primary school! Eventually, we found a place we could call home, an old boat shed down by the harbour.

When my dad first came across the building five years ago, it was just a brick shell, housing a few old broken-down canoes that would never see the water again. It has a large green cast-iron door that opens out onto the water. The back of the club faces on to the main railway track into Dublin city. Outside, it's such an idyllic picture: boats docked on the water, people feeding the swans, the Wicklow mountains in the background. Inside is a different world: there's a cloud of sweat rising up from all those who are training hard, and you can hear my dad shouting at people to push harder.

The buzzer will go off to begin another round of sparring, and there is the noise of skipping ropes clipping the floorboards or gloves pounding off the heavy bags. It smells like sweat and blood. It feels like a boxing club, it has that gritty character about it.

It's small though, and space is tight; the maximum number of people we can train is 20. The facilities there

Doing pads with Dad.

are very basic – it was only after the 2012 World Championships in China that we had our first toilet put in! Before then, we would have to run down the road to the Harbour Bar to use their bathroom.

But this is our home and we love it; this is where Adam Nolan and I poured blood, sweat and tears to qualify for the London Olympics. Bray was the only club in the world with two boxers at London 2012, and the only club ever to have a male and a female boxer representing them in an Olympics. Yeah, we're proud of that and I think it says a lot about my dad's coaching.

On a few occasions I have been away in training camps in countries where the facilities are amazing, where the gyms are purpose-built with all the latest hi-tech equipment, some with three or four rings in the venue. I say to myself: 'Wow, this is great!' But after a week in those surroundings, the novelty wears off and we usually can't wait to get back to our own gym.

Where we are now is the best set-up we've ever had, and it's the first venue where we have ever had a permanent ring, so while it might not be ultra-modern we are grateful for it. After all, when I won my first European title back in 2005 and my first world title the following year, I was training out of the kitchen and the garden shed of my house! Although we had access to our boxing club for

> These were the humble beginnings for me as a boxer, but they have made me grateful for what we now have.

two nights a week, Dad and I used to train the rest of the time in the kitchen and in a freezing bare-block shed he threw up in the back garden of the house.

Dad built the shed himself and he hung a bag in it and kitted it out with weights too. It was 15 feet by 15 feet. When I was younger, Peter and I would sit out there on the bench and watch Dad train. He was always out there hitting the bag or lifting weights. I remember he'd put all the weights on the leg press, and then Peter and I would sit on top, and he would push us and the weights up and down as we sat there making faces at one another. It was such a makeshift gym, but you have to make the best of what you've got. These were the humble beginnings for me as a boxer, but they have made me grateful for what we now have. It also reinforces to me that it's not about the facilities, or the environment (though those things can help), but ultimately a fancy gym can't win you gold medals.

Football

Somewhere along the line, I had to reluctantly give up playing sports that I loved. The two sports that made the cut and survived into my teenage years and early adulthood were football and boxing; it was always going to be a showdown between those two. I loved them both and never really wanted to make the decision to drop one or the other. I did manage to avoid making that decision for years, and competed in both at an international level well into my twenties.

There comes a point in the life of all junior boxers, when you hit 14 or 15 years old, when the punches suddenly start to hurt, and you have to decide whether you're going to take it seriously or not at all.

There is no middle ground. That is why there is a sharp drop-out rate in boxing at about this age. That change, when I started to feel the punches, made me realise that if I was going to stick with this, I was going to have to be more diligent – and that meant that some of my other sporting commitments would have to be cut.

Slowly but surely, all the other sports that I loved began to be dropped in favour of boxing, though I was still clinging tightly to my second love: football. It would be many years later before I was ready to give that up. It was a big risk when I look back, because women's boxing hadn't even been sanctioned in this country yet. To focus my energy on a sport that didn't even exist in Ireland doesn't seem like a smart decision, but I knew somewhere in my heart that I was made for this.

Thank God the risk paid off, and eventually women's boxing became an official sport (after a lot of fighting and campaigning from my parents) so things began to take off for me. It wasn't long before I was getting opportunities to travel and represent Ireland in international boxing tournaments. It was 2005 when I won my first major tournament, I was 18 years old and I was Ireland's first female European boxing champion. The following year, I would retain this title, and I would also travel to New Delhi, India to win the first of my four world titles. Those first couple of years of international boxing were incredible.

My football career was moving along parallel to the boxing. Before long, I found myself straddling two international teams before I was 20 years old. One foot was in boxing, the other in football. In hindsight, something had to give, but I couldn't see it like that then.

I began to realise that in the last few years I was playing football, it wasn't meaning as much to me as it had in previous seasons. In the end, I was doing it almost as a break from the boxing, to get away from the intensity of that sport.

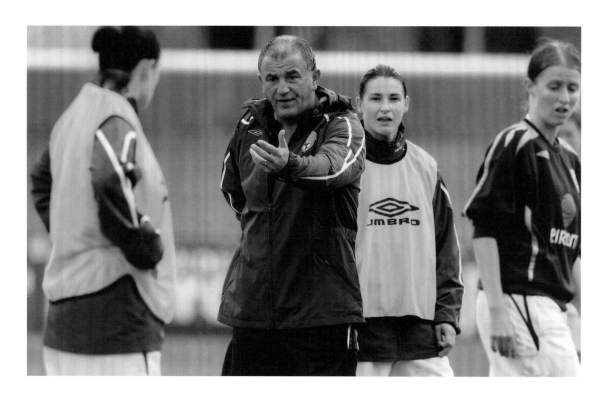

I look on as Noel King delivers his message during training.

But the early years were fantastic for me, and when I first got called up to the Under-17 Ireland team, it was the best day of my life to that point. I was just 13 or 14 years old at the time. A few years later, when I captained the team for the Youth Olympics in Paris, the manager Noel King said to me: 'I know you are not much of a talker, Katie, but you can lead by example.' That stuck with me and it's what I always tried to do. I would lead on the pitch. Someone else could take up the talking role.

At the age of 15, I was selected for the Under-19 squad by manager Sue Ronan, who now manages the senior team. Even though I was so young, I was physically very strong from years of boxing training, so the age gap never seemed to be an issue. During my time with the Under-19 squad, I won the Player of the Year award, an achievement I was very proud of at the time. I was really enjoying playing, and if you had asked me then, playing football professionally was a very real possibility.

My first call-up for the Irish senior squad was when I was about 16 years old. It was Noel King who again selected me. At the time it was a huge ambition of mine to play for the senior team, so this was a real honour. Again, despite my youth, I had no problem competing physically with senior players, but the football was far more technical and tactical than at the under-age levels. For the first year or so, I struggled to find the level but at 19 I made my full international debut for the team.

My first call-up for the Irish senior squad was when I was about 16 years old.

One of the turning points in breaking into the first team was when I played against the American team for Mia Hamm's testimonial. Hamm is a retired American soccer legend, who was the star forward for many years on the United States women's national team. At the time, they were the best football side in the world and Olympic champions. Noel informed me that I was in the starting line-up. I was going to be playing in midfield and Shannon Boxx, one of the world's top midfield players, was playing opposite me. Talk about a challenge! In my mind, I can still see Noel screaming at me constantly from the sidelines. I was so inexperienced, but I wasn't overawed by it. I had looked forward to the contest and in the end I was chuffed with my performance. It was a big game for me personally, even if we did lose 5-0.

There was a great social side to the football, which was probably good for me because boxing can be a lonely sport, not just because it's an individual pursuit but because it demands a very strict lifestyle that doesn't lend itself well to spending weekends in a pub – not that I would have been into that anyway. A lot of my close friends have come from the various football teams that I've played for over the years.

One of my best friends, Susan Byrne, came up through the junior ranks of the Irish teams with me. We were in the Under-17 Ireland side together, then the Under-19 team and then we were both called up to

Driving past Amy McDonald during Ireland's World Cup qualifier against Scotland in May 2006.

the senior team at around the same time. We also played for the same club teams, at Lourdes Celtic, St James's Gate and then Peamount United. Susan travelled over to London for the Games with some of my other friends from football to support me in the ExCeL. They were probably my loudest fans over there!

As I moved into my twenties, juggling two international careers was becoming increasingly difficult. I thought I could manage both, but there was a growing concern from the boxing association about the risk of me picking up a football injury. It was a legitimate worry and I'd never have forgiven myself if I'd missed a big boxing tournament, something I'd spent months preparing for, because I got hurt playing football.

I was trying to cope with a recurring back injury at the time and the kicking action in football would really aggravate it. I went all over the country looking for a physio or a chiropractor to sort it out and eventually found a physio called John Murphy, based in Blackrock, Dublin. He has been with me ever since. He's part of the fantastic team that I depend on.

The clash between the two sports first became apparent while I was trying to prepare for the 2004 European Championships in Riccione, Italy. I had just played football with the Ireland Under-19 team in a European qualifying tournament, which was held in Dublin. We had played three international matches and I also had a cup final with my club team the following week. That was four football matches in the space of ten days – and I was trying to prepare for a boxing tournament at the same time.

The Irish squad were staying in a hotel near Dublin airport and my dad would drive out to me so he could train me in between matches, which was an agreement he had made with the manager,

The clash between the two sports first became apparent while I was trying to prepare for the 2004 European Championships in Riccione, Italy.

> ## Trying to mix the two, the boxing and the football, had finally caught me up.

Sue Ronan. We didn't have anywhere to train, so we would do our sessions in my hotel room. We had to move the bed over to the side and train in the space that was left. It wasn't exactly ideal preparation, but it was our first major boxing championships and we were a bit naïve.

After an intense week with the Irish football team, I went to my first boxing European Championships. I was wrecked, exhausted, emptied. Even though it was my first Europeans, there was an expectation on me since I had recently beaten the world champion Jennifer Ogg. I had gone from being supremely confident to being paralysed with tiredness. Trying to mix the two, the boxing and the football, had finally caught me up. When I stepped through those ropes, I just wasn't myself and I suffered my first loss in the ring. I was devastated at the time, but in retrospect it was a bit of a relief, I had built up such an obsession over protecting my undefeated record that I had started to tense up in the ring. Now I could go back to focusing on my performance.

That loss was a real wake-up call. In my head, I began to realise that I couldn't commit to the two sports at that level any more. But, despite this, I continued to play the football for some more years, eventually winning 19 caps, but I never again let it interfere with my boxing preparations.

I guess it was hard at the time to step away from it – I was always so honoured to play for Ireland whenever I was selected. I loved doing both. What I had to do was put everything into boxing and try to hold on to everything I had in football, playing in crucial international games if my boxing schedule allowed.

The change I made was one of emphasis. Whenever an international match came up, and if I was asked to play, I tried to fit in a couple of club games beforehand to get my sharpness back.

Taking on Marci Miller of the USA during an international in San Diego – July 2006.

But I could only keep this going for so long, as a player I was going downhill. I couldn't keep up the standard, not at international level. I was playing football so sporadically and was trying to come in and compete with girls that were playing week in week out.

My performances on the pitch were becoming increasingly inconsistent. This was frustrating because I used to feel that I had dominated my position in the games I played at international level in the Under-17 and Under-19 age groups. But that was when I was playing regularly.

It inevitably came to that point where basic things, such as my first touch on the ball, were on a slide and getting worse. One day I could have a good game, the next game I could be absolutely terrible.

> I knew what positions I had to take up during the matches, but I didn't have that type of fitness or the stamina in my legs to get there.

The frustration wasn't the only issue in the end, more critically it stopped being enjoyable. I would still give it everything I had and tried to be as physical as I could, tried to look for the ball all of the time and I always pushed to get my tackles in. I knew what positions I had to take up during the matches, but I didn't have that type of fitness or the stamina in my legs to get there. Boxing is a completely different type of fitness from football. In boxing, I compete over four two-minute rounds. A football match is 90 minutes and demands a different set of muscles and stamina.

I was also beginning to arrive late into challenges. I realised that the less frequently I played, the more my timing was off. Not only was I almost injuring myself with some late, mistimed challenges, but on one occasion during a big European qualifier against Italy, I managed to get myself sent off.

Looking back now, I can see the funny side. I had received a yellow card after a late challenge in the first half, but minutes earlier had actually scored a cracking goal putting us 1-0 up at the break. I remember Noel King saying to me at half time: 'Be careful not to get sent off in the second half.' He explained that we couldn't afford to end the game with only ten players on the pitch. Five minutes into the second half, I went in for a challenge, mistimed it again and I got sent off. Noel was understanding about it. After all, he couldn't say a lot as I think he was sent off a few

times himself during his career! But he was right about one thing: we ended up losing the match 4-1.

Over those years, Noel was so accommodating to me. When he knew I had a boxing tournament there was no problem, and when I was available to play he always selected me. It got to the point where I was feeling guilty about being chosen, and I'd think about emailing him to tell him to unpick me because I felt I was taking someone else's place in the squad. Towards the end, my confidence had begun to take a hit and I was reluctant to come in and play. I think Noel knew, but he would still pick me. He knew that at least he would get

Challenging Italy's Alessia Tuttino for the ball in a European Championship qualifier in May 2007. In the return fixture, I received my marching orders.

Evading the sliding challenge from Jayne Ludlow of Arsenal in a friendly in February 2008.

100 per cent out of me, no matter what. The thing was I had speed and I could be really physical and I always worked to get my tackles in. Ultimately that's all I could offer the Irish team: my tenacity and a willingness to be physical.

My last game of football for Ireland was against Kazakhstan in Kazakhstan in September 2009. It was a qualifying game for the 2011 World Cup and we won 2-1. In the end, I was thinking that every football tournament I played was another week I could have spent boxing training, so I knew it was time to put the boots away. I still sometimes get the occasional urge to play, but then it fades. I no longer have the same desire for the game. I can't even remember the last time I watched a match.

At this point I have been away from football for three years or so, and I don't expect to discover any desire to go back playing again. I loved representing my country and it was always a privilege for me. But I knew there was something else out there for me; a personal challenge I could not resist . . . an Olympic dream.

My final game for Ireland, coming on as a substitute against Kazakhstan in September 2009.

CHAPTER 3

GETTING INTO THE RING

At first Dad thought the boxing would blow over.

First Steps in Boxing

As a young athlete, I was a jack-of-all-trades. I played so many sports and I was drawn to different aspects of what each sport offered. But when it came to boxing, I liked everything about it.

The more I became involved in the sport and the more I learned about its demands, the more it captured my attention. It seemed everything about it was hard and required a lot of discipline – and I loved that. It appeared to suit my personality. From an early age I possessed the discipline to push myself to the limits. I've always believed that some of my opponents wouldn't be able to cope with the sacrificial side of the sport in the way I could. I think it has been one of the big factors in my success.

My first memories of boxing were not in a gym but in the kitchen of my house watching my dad training; he was still competing when I was a child. Sometimes he would take a couple of pairs of gloves out to the bank and make out a boundary with four jumpers as a boxing ring. All the lads from the estate would gather around and he would match them up by size and age for a sparring session. By all the lads I mean all the lads and me, of course. They would have been my first sparring sessions.

(*Previous page*) Dad, Lee, Peter and I line up ahead of the time we all boxed on the same card.

I used to mess around a lot in the house too with Peter and Lee, my two older brothers. We would put on my Dad's gloves and pretend to be famous boxers fighting at a big Las Vegas show. We'd even do the ring announcements: 'In the red corner, weighing in at . . .' I would pretend to be Rocky Marciano. I didn't really know who he was, but I knew he was an undefeated champion and that was good enough for me!

Messing around in the kitchen like that might have been all it ever came to were it not for the good old Irish weather. Dad was dropping me off at an athletics meeting one Tuesday night on his way to the boxing club in Enniskerry where he trained. It was lashing with rain and because of the weather, the athletics was cancelled, so Dad had to bring me training with him. And that's how my boxing career began – it was as simple as that.

As a kid, my boxing gloves seemed huge.

With brother Lee.

As a child I would pretend to be Rocky Marciano, but here it is Rocky Balboa on the receiving end.

This was my first time setting foot in a boxing club and yet it all seemed so natural. I had a great intuition for how to stand the right way and how to shift my body weight when I punched, probably from years of watching my dad hitting the bag out in our shed or shadow boxing in our kitchen. I remember sparring that night and not being nervous at all, just excited. It's easier to start at that age because the punches don't hurt, and the gloves were nearly bigger than me.

It wasn't until I was around ten years old that I started going to the club regularly. By this stage my dad was no longer competing and he had opened his own club across from our estate. Lee was already involved in boxing and Peter started around the same time as me. So we were all in the club training together. In my first club show, we all boxed on the same card: my two brothers, Dad and me. I think it was a first, at least in this country.

(*Right*) In my first exhibition match I was up against a young lad called Michael Hart.

From then, it blossomed and grew: I became known as the little girl boxer. Some of the local media were curious at the idea of a little girl boxing and it seemed to spark a bit of controversy. I was interviewed by some of the local newspapers and my mam went on a well-known radio talk-show to defend my right to box. It didn't seem unusual to me; I didn't understand what all the controversy was about. As a child, the way I saw it: my dad and my brothers boxed, so why couldn't I?

The first time I set foot in a boxing club it all seemed so natural. I had a great intuition for how to stand and how to shift my body weight when I punched.

> Dad had never intended any of us to box. It came about naturally. People would complain that it was too dangerous for a girl, but at that age I wasn't getting hurt in the ring.

Dad had never intended any of us to box. It came about naturally. From seeing him train and tagging along with him to the boxing club, we were all sucked in. People would complain that it was too dangerous for a girl, but at that age I wasn't getting hurt in the ring. Obviously as time went by, the lads I was training with started getting bigger and stronger, and the punches began to hurt, but the change was gradual.

I learned to adapt my style so I didn't take as many shots. When I look back on those early days, I had a very different style to today: I was all aggression. I would just throw hundreds of punches every round without any real method. As I got older, I soon learned the value of a good defence! My style has evolved over the years, and I'm now a more cautious boxer. My dad always coached me not to give away any easy points, but if I need to throw caution to the wind and be aggressive, I have that side to me too.

At first Dad thought the boxing would blow over for me, and I'd focus on something else as my main sporting discipline. In truth, up until my mid-teens, I still saw it as something that added to my football, an extra training outlet, if you like. It helped to give me a strength advantage over the other girls I was playing against. It continued to be an important factor right throughout my football career, especially when making the step up to the Irish senior squad. It wasn't a one-way street, though: the football complemented my boxing too, since my leg strength and footwork have always been a crucial part of my boxing style.

Working with Dad

Dad's been asked before how our relationship works, trying to play the role of coach and father to his daughter. Sometimes the lines can get blurred between father, coach and manager – that's inevitable – but the bottom line for me is that nobody could have my best interests at heart in the same way as a parent. There is nobody I would trust more to coach or manage me.

I was always a daddy's girl growing up. He took me everywhere: to football, to the running club, to the boxing club and even to work! I'd even help him out with the wallpapering and jobs around the house. I think that by spending so much time with him I got my competitive spirit from him – we both really hate losing. So much so that it can cause a bit of tension between us during our post-training table-tennis matches.

For as long as I can remember, he always poured so much time and energy into me. We would spend hours playing football together at the local pitches during the long summer evenings and we would run together all the time, too. He would go to every match I played and every race I ran, even when it meant missing work. And now he is my full-time coach, so we spend large parts of every day together. When I wanted to take up boxing competitively, there was probably a part of him that was reluctant, on a few occasions he said to me: 'You don't "play" boxing, you play football.' Boxing is a serious sport so if you're going to do it, you don't take it lightly or you will end up suffering the consequences in the ring.

As a father, he gets so nervous when I step into the ring. But he knows my ability better than anybody, so although he gets nervous I don't think he's ever worried about me getting hurt, with one exception. When I was 17, I fought against the Canadian world

> Jennifer Ogg was the best boxer in the world, almost twice my age at the time and a hardened veteran of the sport. I was a 17-year-old with almost no experience at international level.

champion, Jennifer Ogg, for the first time. The bout took place in Cascia, Italy, as part of the Torneo Italia Women's Tournament. I think Dad had a nightmare before I was due to take her on, and he wanted to pull me out of the fight. She was the best boxer in the world, almost twice my age at the time and a hardened veteran of the sport. I was a 17-year-old with almost no experience at international level. I remember we had this serious talk the day before the fight to talk through whether or not he was going pull me out of the fight, but I was thinking: 'Don't do it. These are the big fights you dream about – boxing against the world champion. You can't pull me out of this fight.'

He actually rang the Irish Amateur Boxing Association (IABA) in Dublin and told them he didn't think he could allow me to box in this one, because I was still so young. They argued that it would be a good experience for me; after all, it was a major international tournament, but then I wasn't their daughter! The deciding factor for Dad was the quality of the sparring partners I had worked with in the club. He recognised that, although Ogg was physically so strong, she was not as strong as the lads that I was sparring with, nor as fast.

Every week when I trained, I was in against better, faster and stronger fighters than Ogg, no disrespect intended. That's how Dad worked it through and made the decision I should take the fight. We went for one of our walks and were talking about it and it just clicked. He was going to let me box. As a coach, I don't think he ever doubted my abilities, but as a father he was concerned about his teenage girl going up against a more powerful and more experienced fighter.

By the time we stepped into the ring together, Ogg had some 200 fights under her belt, while I had had five international fights.

I think she had been unbeaten for a few years. Physically, she was a power-house. Honestly though, her reputation didn't faze me. On the one hand, I was a young aspiring boxer and so to be in the same tournament as the world champion was a privilege. On the other hand, she was the person I most wanted to box when I got to the tournament and saw her name in the draw. I remember saying to my mam: 'I hope I draw Jennifer Ogg – that's the fight I want.'

My dad was worried about the age difference, and the fact that I was a young girl with no real muscle development at that stage, while this girl was built like a tank. But I wasn't afraid; there was probably an element of naivety in it, but I was convinced I could beat her.

World champion Jennifer Ogg evades a punch during our bout in Italy – it was a major step forward for me.

> **That fight proved to be the first big breakthrough in my career. I remember it well. Dad told me exactly what to do.**

I was determined to beat her. At the end of the day, I had nothing to lose: she was the current world champion while I was just an Irish girl new on the scene.

That fight proved to be the first big breakthrough in my career. I remember it well. Dad told me exactly what to do. He advised that whenever the referee told us to break, I should always walk behind him, because Ogg was always quick on the attack after there had been a break. She would overwhelm her opponents with this constant pressure, but if I stood behind the referee it would prevent her getting at me immediately, giving me some relief and breaking up her momentum. I remember his advice so clearly. So during our fight, every time the referee said break I would walk behind his back and she couldn't get to me at once.

The tactics were flawless as usual. I remember every instruction Dad gave me. I also recall him saying: 'Every time you feel your calf brush against the rope, push her back to the centre of the ring.' All of the things he told me to do, I executed perfectly. I was a sponge taking in all of his advice, and as a result I beat her pretty convincingly. At that stage of my career, it was a huge win.

In hindsight, you might ask why Dad had his doubts about my ability to cope with her strength, as I was always sparring against men who were physically very strong. But that tension between coach and father is something that he constantly has to deal with. In some ways, it has its advantages, because the father in him will always be concerned when I fight, he will never take a fight for granted, no matter what titles I have won. On the other hand, big fights for my dad are demanding and he is usually emotionally and physically shattered afterwards.

Planning a Fight

My win against Ogg changed everything for me. I began to believe the sky was the limit. That victory also made me realise something else: I needed Dad in my corner.

When it comes to preparing me, Dad goes the extra mile. I don't know anybody as meticulous as him in the build-up to a fight. He will study videos hour after hour and write down what tactics I should adopt to counter any fighter I might come up against. It is time-consuming. He shows complete and utter dedication to making sure no stone is left unturned. That is the difference I see between having him in my corner and somebody else.

I land a punch on Jennifer Ogg on the way to a great victory over the world champion.

> I had had a very gruelling semi-final against the American boxer Queen Underwood the day before the final. The fight developed into a toe-to-toe punch-up.

To give you some idea of what I mean, Dad will usually have videos of every fight that my opponent has fought over the last ten years. He will study and analyse them all if he has to. He will assess the different tactics my opponent has adopted in her previous fights, and how her approach changes according to her opponent's style. He does all this to ensure we are prepared for any likely possibility. He will always have a clear plan devised for me before I go into the ring and I always trust that it is the right one. Of course, however well we plan ahead, nothing can ever be set in concrete, because sometimes I'll have to adapt to my opponent's tactics.

In boxing, there is a conventional wisdom about how to handle certain styles and most coaches abide by that 'wisdom'. But Dad tends to think outside the box, and his unconventional tactics have helped me win a lot of important fights, never more so than the final of the 2010 World Championships in Barbados against Cheng Dong from China.

I had had a very gruelling semi-final against the American boxer Queen Underwood the day before the final. I had been beating the American comfortably after two rounds, but the fight had developed into a toe-to-toe punch-up and I had put everything into building up my early lead. Gradually, the momentum began to swing in the favour of Underwood and she managed to claw her way back into the fight and was in fact leading with 30 seconds left on the clock.

I had nothing left in the tank. I remember glancing over at my dad in the corner and he signalled to me that I was a point down, while my family were on their knees in the stands praying for a breakthrough in the closing seconds. I nodded at my dad as if to acknowledge that I knew what I needed to do, so I dug deep, deeper than I've ever

dug before, and found the strength to let off some big combinations in the last ten seconds. Every punch was sharp and the judges agreed – I won the fight by two points.

That victory took me through to meet Cheng Dong in the final. She is a very tall fighter and she makes great use of her height by moving around the ring and boxing long range. As we prepared for the contest the night before, Dad told me the way he thought that the fight would pan out. He was convinced that Cheng Dong was going

Queen Underwood pushed me hard in the semi-final of the 2010 World Championship – but I won through in the end.

Dad made sure I got my tactics just right for my world title decider in 2010 against Cheng Dong.

to take an aggressive approach, that she would try take the fight to me. But most pundits would have disagreed, because that was not the way she usually boxed. They would have expected her to be moving around the ring, waiting for me to come to her so she could counter with those long arms of hers. Because he had studied her previous fights in such detail, he was able to tell me everything that was going to happen in the fight. His predictions were so accurate that it got to the point where it was as though I had already seen the fight in my head. Everything he said happened. The tactics we had prepared were perfect: she came to me, as Dad had predicted, and I was ready for her.

The same thing happened in the final of the European Championships in Rotterdam

> Because he had studied her previous fights in such detail, he was able to tell me everything that was going to happen in the fight.

in 2011. On that occasion, I was up against Sofya Ochigava, which is always a tactical fight. She and I are excellent counter-punchers, so neither of us is particularly willing to commit first, which makes for a boring fight for the average spectator but a fascinating fight for the purists. Dad thought that the fight would be so tentative that the referee would be forced to warn us both for not throwing enough punches. He told me not to worry about the referee's warnings and to hold my nerve as long as I needed. He knew it would be like a poker match, as we would both be looking for a chink in each other's armour before trying anything too dramatic, so he warned me that I'd have to be patient. Again, everything happened just as he had predicted, even down to the referee stopping the fight to caution us for being too passive. Being able to give the right tactics like that time after time takes hours of preparation and study.

The moment of triumph: I am crowned world champion for the third time in 2010.

Getting the Preparations Right

Dad plans out my training programme for the year with just the same meticulous attention to detail. He will write down schedules, making sure that every cycle is perfect, down to the running sessions, the weight training, the recovery, everything. It is all planned months in advance, because of his commitment to me as a father and his passion for boxing as a coach.

Because we are so close, he also understands me better than any other coach; he knows the way my body reacts and behaves, and knows my moods and disposition. When we are in serious competition I am incredibly obsessive in my approach to fights, which I don't think any other coach would understand. I make an effort to exclude myself from everyone so that I can be single-minded and focused on the task ahead.

To give you one example of what I mean, in the Olympic Village this summer I always had my breakfast on my own in my room. My mental preparation starts as soon as I wake up, so I don't like talking too much – besides I'm not exactly good company on the day of a fight. After breakfast, Dad and I would go for one of our pre-fight walks to discuss tactics, as this has always been a part of our pre-fight ritual. He is the only one I like to talk about the fight with, as he has a unique way of communicating tactics to me because he knows the way I think when it comes to boxing. In an ideal world, I think all boxers would have their own club coaches with them at important championships, because those coaches have worked with them since they were kids and they know what makes them tick. This obviously isn't feasible for most boxers, so I recognise that we are fortunate to be able to do it this way. Thank God we are in that position.

There is no doubt that I have a very special relationship with my dad. I know that I can trust his advice for me without any question.

(*Right*) Appearing in the Lucozade Sport YES campaign, which also featured Tinie Tempah and Blink 182 drummer Travis Barker.

For me, there is something very relaxing about being able to go to bed the night before a fight, knowing that I have complete, 100 per cent trust in the person that is going to be telling me what to do in my corner.

> It is the partnership we have, and the fact that we completely understand each other, that enables me always to go into the ring relaxed and fully prepared.

There have been times early in my international career when I was away at tournaments and Dad hasn't been picked as my coach. In those cases, I was completely stressed by the approach of other coaches. It was not that they had done anything wrong; it was just that they couldn't understand the way I like to mentally prepare for a fight and that I get stressed if there is a lack of attention to detail.

It's not that I'm mentally fragile – quite the opposite, I have always had great mental strength – it's just that I believe the boxer should be thinking about the fight ahead, not about the logistical details. For example, I will be annoyed if a team member is late to get on the bus that takes us to the boxing venue, because this means that the planned schedule is knocked out slightly. And now my mind is not on my fight but on getting to the venue on time. If the bus is due to leave at ten o'clock, then you should be there by ten o'clock, and not a minute or two minutes later. The same goes for training: if it starts at 11 that is when you should be there, ready to start on time.

People might think that that's extreme, but to me the little details matter, and anything that helps me in the ring, no matter how small, is not extreme. Thankfully, most of the team that travels with us know by now that I have a very intense way of preparing for fights so they're not offended by my moods on fight day.

Another great advantage of having Dad in my corner is that I'd never find myself in a situation where I'd have to look for the coach when I wanted to warm up. These things are absolutely vital for a boxer. I don't want to be looking around for my coach, only for him to tell me I'm not on for an hour and a half, so I should wait for a while before beginning my warm-up routine. I know in my own mind when I need to warm up. It is an individual thing. That is the difference between having Dad there and anyone else, and it has been crucial in my success. It is the partnership we have, and the fact that we completely understand each other, that enables me always to go into the ring relaxed and fully prepared for what might lie ahead.

Both my parents, in fact, have been crucial in my success. When I'm away at a competition, I only ever have to think about the fight ahead of me, as everything else is looked after by them. This applies to the big things, like prayer and tactics, as well as the small, trivial things. For example, if I want a bottle of water and it is on the other side of the hotel room, Mam or Dad will get it for me before I even have a chance to get off the bed. If I mentioned that I was peckish, they would run down to the nearest shop to get me something. They make such sacrifices for my sake. As far as they're concerned, they don't want me wasting energy on anything other than the fight. So when I'm away, I focus on winning, and Mam and Dad are willing to do everything else they can to help make it happen.

Before a fight, most people want to warm up for about 15 minutes, but I prefer a much longer warm-up, and Dad knows that. He even plans the warm-up in advance. Five fights before I am on, we start walking and talking; four fights before we might start a general warm-up, just loosening up the muscles. With three fights to go, we will be doing shadow boxing; then two fights before we might do some light pad-work and so with one fight to go, I just think and focus on the bout ahead. We have the warm-up down to a science.

We will always have someone watching the previous bouts in case a fight is stopped early and we have less time to warm up. If that happens, then we have to adapt. We need all of that information brought to us, because it's important that Dad is with me the whole time so he can't be constantly running out to check what is going on in the arena. You really do need this level of professionalism from your team, and I'm blessed to have a group around me that understands this.

With the top Turkish fighter, Gulsum Tatar.

I recognise that our attitude can make it difficult for anyone who travels with us on a boxing trip. We know that what works for us is to be intense people. That's not to say that we don't have the craic and a laugh when we are in competition, but we do want everything to be professional. Some people think we're too serious. I remember when I won my semi-final in the World Championships in China earlier this year, having also secured my Olympic qualification earlier in the tournament. One of the British coaches said to me: 'Katie, it's OK, you're allowed to smile!' I replied: 'I'll smile when I'm on the podium tomorrow with the gold medal around my neck!' I've said it before: I enjoy my tournaments by winning them, and there is no other way. Everyone on my team lightens up and smiles at the end when the job is done. That is the only way I understand, the way that I think it should be done.

A few times in the early days, Dad wasn't always picked as the coach to travel with me to tournaments. But I think the High Performance Unit, who look after an elite group of boxers in Ireland, soon realised they were splitting up a winning team. There was something special about him being in my corner and I was always a better boxer with him there. I was like that even as a child: I always felt more confident when he was watching, whether in my corner during a fight or on the touchline during a football match.

> There is something special about Dad being in my corner and I was always a better boxer with him there. I was like that even as a child.

Working with Other Coaches

The first time I boxed without Dad beside me, I was beaten by the Turkish fighter Gulsum Tatar in the European Union Championships 2006 in Sardinia. Mentally, I just wasn't right – I couldn't wait for the fight to be over, which was weird for me. I was nervous and tense all day, simply because my dad was not there. I needed him around. It's not that the other coaches weren't competent, but it was a trust thing. I know I can trust him in a way that is never going to be the same with anyone else.

With Dad, left, and Zauri Antia during the EU Championships final against Karolina Graczyk in Katowice, Poland, 4 June 2011.

Dad and Zauri Antia celebrate with me after my semi-final victory in the World Championships in Qinhuangdao, China, May 2012.

My next competition was the Norway Box Cup and again Dad was left out, with two other coaches picked instead. Then one of them pulled out, but still they didn't choose Dad, going for an alternative option. But when the replacement also had to drop out a week before we went out there, they finally asked Dad if he would go. I was so relieved that he was back in my corner. Eventually, I won the tournament and I also got the award for best boxer. With my dad there with me, I was back to my best.

After that episode, they realised that it was going to be hard to separate the two of us. Gary Keegan, who was the High Performance

Unit director at the time, was the first to admit it wasn't the right decision to break us apart. He had been doing only what he thought was right, and trying to find ways to get the best out of me at the time. He believed that if I worked with different coaches, it might give me new insights. I can see where he was coming from, but it just didn't

Training with Dad at Bray Boxing Club. Working with him brings out the best in me.

work for me. We have a great relationship with Gary. I know the decisions he was making had my best interests at heart. He was also one of the people who supported me and women's boxing from the very beginning.

These days, my schedule is worked out by Dad in conjunction with the High Performance Unit. He is employed by the Irish Sports Council to coach me alone, and is the technical adviser to female boxing in Ireland. Without doubt, this is the system that has worked best for us. Not only because he knows me better than anyone else, but because he has the same obsessive approach to his preparation as I do to mine. When I qualified for the London Olympics at the World Championships in China, my dad started planning for the Olympics on the flight home. I don't think anyone could argue with the results!

To have my dad coach me makes perfect practical sense too. The other national coaches have to travel to tournaments regularly with the men's teams, so there would be no one in the national gym in Dublin to train with. Instead, we do most of our work in our club in Bray and try to make a weekly trip into the national gym to train with national team there. Coming up to a major championship, we will go in more often for specific sparring partners who might have a style similar to a potential opponent.

There's a good reason why it makes sense for me to do the bulk of my training in Bray, rather than in Dublin. Women box four two-minute rounds while the men box three three-minute rounds. So when I'm in the national gym with the lads, I tend to box three-minute rounds. It may not seem much, but there is a big difference between two-minute and three-minute rounds, as the three-minute rounds require a much bigger aerobic capacity, while the pace of the

> It makes sense for me to do the bulk of my training in Bray, rather than in Dublin. Women box four two-minute rounds while the men box three three-minute rounds.

Dad watches on during a training session in Bray.

With Darren O'Neill, who captained the Irish boxing team at the Olympics, and super bantamweight Carl Frampton, who remains undefeated since turning pro back in 2009.

round wouldn't be as hard as a typical two-minute round. When I am sparring against the Irish lads, their strength really comes through in the longer rounds. During the last minute of a round, they seem to pull away and get stronger and stronger. It's good to occasionally box the three-minute rounds to improve my aerobic fitness, but in general it's better to train as specific to my needs as possible. So Dad organises and develops the training plan for me and uses the sparring in our club in Bray to suit what's right for me.

> It's good to occasionally box the three-minute rounds to improve my aerobic fitness, but in general it's better to train as specific to my needs as possible.

The IABA and the High Performance Unit have been very supportive of me, and I've been grateful for their help. If we need nutritionists or physiotherapy or extra sparring, they have organised it for us. They also battled hard for me to get into some training camps in Italy, Germany, Ukraine and Georgia that were exclusively for men, and I was the only female boxer there. Those training camps were so important in my preparation for the Games.

The High Performance boxing squad with coaches Billy Walsh (left) and Zauri Antia (right).

CHAPTER 4

FLYING THE FLAG
FOR IRELAND

This was a once-in-a-lifetime opportunity.

Getting in the Mood

My Olympics began with one million megawatts of brightness from the Olympic Stadium lights and the smiles and flashes of 80,000 people about to hammer down on us as I waited with the rest of Team Ireland outside the gates of the stadium. My team-mate Paddy Barnes is jokingly trying to rip the Irish flag out of my hands, at least I think he's joking. After all, he had made it publicly known that he wanted the honour of being the flag-bearer for his country.

The mood among the Irish team on the night of the opening ceremony was amazing. We were full of anticipation and excitement, as no one had started competing, and there were also some pre-tournament nerves masquerading as giddiness. At the centre of most of the banter and messing was, of course, our favourite light flyweight, Paddy Barnes.

The forecast that night was that there might be some scattered showers and the other lads on the team were winding up Paddy, saying: 'Paddy you have it, you've got the carrying job you wanted.' Then they pulled out an umbrella and said: 'Here you go, you can carry this and if it rains you open it and hold it over Katie's head to keep her dry while she carries the flag.'

(*Previous page*) Carrying the flag for Ireland at the London Olympic opening ceremony, 27 July 2012. It was a proud moment.

When he gave up on trying to wrestle the flag from me, he showed off his entrepreneurial skills by writing in large letters on a cardboard sign: 'Open for sponsors.' He wasn't going to let the opportunity pass. He told me he was going to hold it up for the cameras when we walked around the stadium. My club-mate and fellow Olympian Adam Nolan also had a sign, but he went with the more sentimental message, 'Hello Ma.' I think he held it up for two seconds and then hid it out of embarrassment. Paddy on the other hand, carried his around without a second thought. I don't think he knows the meaning of the word embarrassment. He did manage to capture the attention of the media and it was all over the papers the next day.

Paddy Barnes holds up his sponsorship sign at the Olympic opening ceremony alongside fellow boxer, Michael Conlan.

Paddy had an ally in all things mischievous in his fellow Belfast boxer, Michael Conlan. They seemed to spend all their free time during the Olympics trying to come up with new ways to mess with people, and for these two lads, the closer to the bone a joke is, the better. A few days after the opening ceremony, we were all in the ExCeL Arena cheering on Paddy through his first win of the competition. Afterwards, I went over to congratulate him and said: 'Well done, Paddy. You were really brilliant.'

He replied: 'Yeah, yeah, thanks Katie. Let me show you a picture I took this week.'

So he went away to get his phone and came back to show me a picture of himself and the world number two in my weight division, Sofya Ochigava, the Russian with whom I've had a sharp boxing rivalry over the last few years and who I eventually met in the Olympic final.

Sharing a joke with Paddy Barnes and Michael Conlan at the IABA Irish Olympic boxing squad Q&A session, National Stadium, Dublin, 15 August 2012. Their humour helped the team so much.

In the photo, he had his arms around her and was grinning away with a massive smile and giving the thumbs up. 'I was looking for her all week,' he said.

I replied, half joking, half serious: 'What are you taking a picture of her for, you traitor?'

'Yeah, she's my favourite boxer,' he said with a cheeky smile – anything to wind me up.

In fact it was Michael Conlan who started the joke of having photographs taken with a team-mate's main rival. Early in the campaign he got a picture of himself with the Chinese flyweight boxer Shiming Zou. The two of them were smiling and Michael had his thumbs up. He knew that Zou had beaten Paddy in the semi-final in Beijing four years previously on the way to picking up gold. Paddy hadn't yet had his chance for revenge, which made it all the more cruel when Michael produced the photograph with his new best friend Zou. At least I had a winning record over Ochigava, so I was able to find the funny side, but Paddy had a score to settle with Zou.

It would be another few days before I would step through the ropes for my first Olympic fight, so it was good to have the team around me for some light-hearted banter before I 'switched on' for the competition.

Training in Assisi

I had spent only one day in the athletes' village before the opening ceremony where I had the privilege of carrying the Irish flag. I had flown in from Dublin the day before with Dad. Prior to that, we'd been out to Assisi in Italy with the rest of the Irish team. It was a gorgeous place for a pre-Olympic training camp, home of that great man of God, St Francis, and a place full of beautiful monasteries and churches. But sadly I never get the chance to enjoy these places properly; we were there to prepare.

Assisi was my boot camp before London and physically it turned out to be one of the cruellest weeks of the year. Each session we did we'd lose three kilos in weight, because in Italy during the month of July you can fry eggs on car bonnets. We see-sawed in weight each day, as the scales told us we'd lost too much fluids from training so we had to rehydrate before our next afternoon session. As if the heat outside wasn't bad enough, our gym had no air conditioning so it was like training in an over-sized sauna – the whole thing felt like torture.

While we were out there, we had a strict routine. For me, each morning began with a weigh-in at seven. Then at ten, I'd spar ten gruelling rounds of two and a half minutes each, before working pads and doing other drills until the session finally came to a close at 11.30. The afternoon wasn't any easier, and on many of the days I found myself back on a football pitch, but not to kick a ball around unfortunately. Instead, Dad would mark out 600 metres, which I would run a number of times with Dad pushing me to run each one in under two minutes. These kind of sessions take you to the edge of yourself, mentally and physically. We trained like this twice a day for six days. I was strong and fit before I arrived at the training camp, but by the time I left beautiful Assisi I was close to reaching my peak.

The lads had gone straight from Assisi to the Olympic Village, but we didn't fancy that because it was too long a wait before my first fight. So we went to Bray for a week, back to home comforts. My first fight wasn't until the second week of the Games, and I needed about a week or ten days of tapering and light training to maintain my weight. I don't train hard right up to the week of a competition, but allow my body recover for that time before trying to peak for the fights. It's still not an easy period, though, because at this stage, I'm usually not eating as much as I'd like to in an effort to knock off the last couple of kilos to make my 60kg weight division.

Flying the Flag

Because of the different starting times of the competitions, it meant my preparations were out of sync with the men. Boxing for them began on 28 July, but I wasn't scheduled to meet Natasha Jonas or Queen Underwood until 6 August. The men would have been tapering and would have finished the heavy gym work while I was still involved in intense training and heavy sparring, so there was no real benefit for me travelling to London at the same time as them. I was working to a schedule that was slightly behind them.

> Whatever my reservations, I knew if I didn't carry the Irish flag that I would have regretted it. The ceremony turned out to be one of the best experiences of my life.

In the end, Dad and I decided not to go to London until ten days before my opening contest and probably would have stayed at home even longer, were it not for the fact that I was the flag-bearer in the opening ceremony and I had my first weigh-in for the competition.

When the president of the Olympic Council of Ireland, Pat Hickey, had rung up Dad to ask if I would be interested in being the Irish flag-bearer for the ceremony, I appreciated that it was a great honour to be asked, but I didn't say yes immediately. I had a couple of reservations. First, I was conscious that Paddy really wanted to carry the flag, but there was no guarantee that if I had turned down the honour, he would be next on the list. Second, I was concerned that it might interfere with my routine and programme and I wasn't going to let anything upset my performances. So I discussed it with my family and we decided that this was a once-in-a-lifetime opportunity and I'd be crazy not to take it. Whatever my reservations, I knew if I didn't carry the Irish flag that I would have regretted it. The ceremony turned out to be one of the best experiences of my life.

Leading the Irish team round the Olympic Stadium was a great honour and a wonderful experience.

These were also my first official steps in London 2012, the first time I had properly dipped my toe into the Olympic Games.

That night, almost the whole team walked together up to the stadium. Unfortunately, some of the athletes were competing the next day so they couldn't come along. It's a long ceremony that can be draining if you have to compete soon after. I was sharing an apartment with the swimmers Melanie Nocher, Grainne Murphy and Sycerika McMahon, and they couldn't make the ceremony because their event was the following day. That was a tough break for them, but they had a great attitude about it, and as I was leaving the apartment I could tell they were excited for me and proud of the fact that I was carrying the flag. It was great to see their team spirit.

As we got closer to the Olympic Stadium, there were thousands of people lining the streets to see the teams file past, and it was then that I really picked up on the breadth and dimensions of the greatest show on earth and realised that the whole world would be watching us that night.

These were also my first official steps in London 2012, the first time I had properly dipped my toe into the Olympic Games. Everything else I'd done earlier in the year, from the World Championships in China to Assisi, and earlier in my life going back to the Tin Can and those first sparring sessions on the bank through to my first shaky teenage steps in international boxing, they were all leading to this and what would unfold over the coming days.

As we moved towards the Olympic Stadium, I was aware that this was the beginning of a new journey for me. In many ways I was extremely proud that I had played my part in getting my sport to the London Games. After women's boxing was accepted into the Olympics, I knew the path was clear for me to try to achieve my dream of Olympic gold, but here in the middle of the throngs of enthusiastic, buzzing Londoners I was feeling it more, almost touching it.

National colours were hanging everywhere in the Olympic Village, where the teams had marked their territorial boundaries. Giant six- and seven-storey flags were draped from some of the balconies. I remember seeing building-sized Union flags, the black and yellow of Belgium, the red of Turkey, and the yellow and green colours of Australia pulled like skirts around the tower blocks.

From the Olympic bus lanes and the special air-conditioned javelin train that flashed fans from King's Cross to Stratford in minutes to the official purple colour of the Games wrapped around every pole and on every bus and seemingly at times all across London itself, the spirit of the Games was reaching everyone, including me.

There was a very real sense that it was the whole city of London that was hosting the Olympics and not just one small area in the East End. No matter where you went in the city, you couldn't escape the fact that something unique and important was taking place. London had taken the Olympics and shaken them into life, and here we were on the verge of walking right into the eye of the storm in the Olympic Stadium itself.

Before we got on to the track, the Irish team gathered together at one of the main gates, and this is where I was first handed the Irish flag. What a moment! Minutes later, we marched into the madness. As we waited to go in, I could peek through and see that the whole place was alive with people and utterly jammed.

The wait to enter the stadium had seemed like an eternity. For the previous hours before the athletes came in, Danny Boyle's 'Isles of Wonder' had played out, reflecting the themes and priorities of the Games, based on sport, inspiration and youth.

There were no instructions given to me as to what to do on the march, but then it wasn't as though it was complicated to keep up with the team ahead. So as I walked into the arena, I blindly followed the person in front of me hoping there wasn't a 'wrong' way to wave a flag, and if there was, hopefully I was doing it right.

(*Overleaf*) Danny Boyle's 'Isles of Wonder' plays out at the opening ceremony.

> All I can really remember was taking pride in the fact that we were in the middle of this enormous world spectacle.

I must admit that all I can really remember as we walked around waving and smiling at the crowds in the stadium was taking pleasure and pride in the fact that we were all in the middle of this enormous world spectacle involving 204 teams. There were representatives from every one of them in the stadium, and it was daunting to think that as many as a billion people were watching in from all over the planet.

We were looking up at the crowd, who seemed to be looking down on us from an incredible height. The lads were taking pictures with their phones and videoing each other. People were phoning their mums and girlfriends and waving at the television cameras. And of course Paddy had his piece of cardboard in the air with personal details for sponsors. It was very relaxed and we tried to take it all in.

Over by the VIPs, there was a forest of poles with the flags of all the nations hanging limply as there was hardly a breeze in the stadium. In among the dignitaries, I could see Seb Coe and Jacques Rogge, the president of the International Olympic Committee, along with dozens of other guests. On we walked.

After we'd gone around the stadium, teams trailed out of the arena while the flag-bearers remained in the centre of the track. The spectacular finale of the event saw the Olympic cauldron, which was formed from 204 copper petals representing the competing nations coming together in London for the Games, ignited by seven young torchbearers. It was sensational to watch and even better to be part of it.

One of the last things I remember is the fireworks exploding into the sky from around the edges of the stadium, which gave the effect of red criss-crosses that reached far up into the sky. Outside there were tens of thousands watching the grand finale.

The Olympic cauldron forms as the 204 copper petals of the competing nations converge.

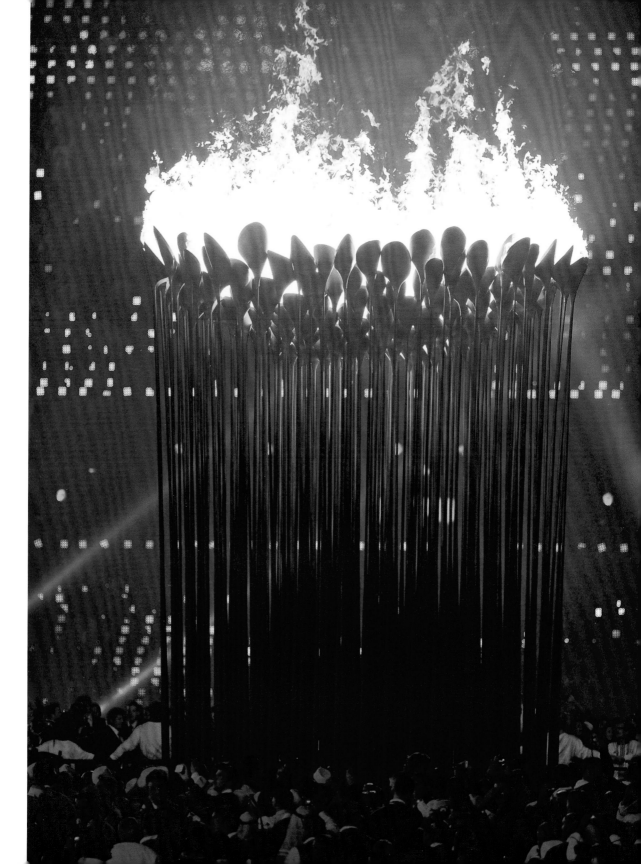

> I thought about the desire and ambition I had had as a child; now that dream was colliding with the present reality of standing in the Olympic Stadium with the London skyline ablaze.

I thought about the desire and ambition I had had as a child; now that dream was colliding with the present reality of standing in the Olympic Stadium with the London skyline ablaze. I was finally part of the Olympic Games!

It was a special night and I was delighted that I had taken the right decision to be a part of it. If I hadn't already been consumed by the thought of winning a medal before that night, then leaving the stadium there was no doubt it was the only thing that mattered to me. Those dreams I had as a child of winning a gold medal were not only still alive in my mind, but they seemed to take on even greater importance after the power and scale of the ceremony.

It was the early hours of the morning when I finally walked out of the stadium, athletes and public together, and by the time I got back to the Olympic Village I was tired but buzzing and now very much alive to what lay ahead.

Getting Ready for Action

We had originally planned to go back to Bray the day after the opening ceremony. But Dad and I decided to stay in the Olympic Village rather than face the journey back to Dublin, mainly because I hate flying. I'm a nervous wreck on planes and although I've flown all around the world, I still find it very stressful. But it comes with the territory of an international boxer so I grin and bear it.

Also, the advantage of staying was that it meant we would have more time to get used to the village and we'd also have a chance to go down to the boxing venue in the ExCeL Arena to get familiar with

(*Previous page*) As the spectacular firework finale of the opening ceremony went off, I knew I was ready for action.

the surroundings there. As the week unfolded, the Olympic Village was an interesting environment, full of the anticipation and the energy of athletes from around the world, but it took some time for me to acclimatise to it.

Dad and I have always given plenty of thought to the way to do things, in terms of travel, accommodation and the best way for me to prepare for any competition. My apartment in the village was comfortable and modern, but most of the places we go to for tournaments and training are usually pretty basic. For example, during the last World Championships in China, we stayed in the dorms of a football school. That was fine, but I couldn't wait to get home, back to Bray.

On that occasion, we decided to fly first-class going over to China. It was the first time we'd done so for a tournament. We realised the benefits of flying first-class following a trip to Los Angeles earlier in the year with one of our sponsors, as my legs weren't as stiff and I took less time to recover from the long flight. I see it as a little one per cent help, and when you add up all the one per cents you get from taking care of the little details, it could be the difference between being on the podium or not. We'll do the same going to Canada for the next World Championships in 2014. It doesn't make the experience of flying any less worrying, but at least it is much more comfortable, and my recovery time at the other end is quicker.

Dad and I are usually the first people from any country to arrive at tournaments, so living in the Olympic Village for more than a week before my first fight was nothing new to either of us. We always prefer doing it this way, as it gives us the comfort of getting familiar with the surroundings, which is important. I like to know where things are and how they work, so I don't stress over them immediately before a bout.

Even in the last European Championships in Rotterdam, all of the teams got there three days after we did. We'd already organised the training facilities for the Irish team in advance of their arrival.

> The noise outside was deafening. I definitely struggled to adapt to the buzz where we were.

For me, it's all about getting the little one per cents again. Sometimes, we have even arrived at venues before the organisers expect us, which has caused a bit of confusion in the past.

We have found over the years that if the entire team arrives together into a hotel in a foreign country, it can become a battle for rooms. It turns into every man for himself, or every woman for herself. There's usually one hotel and everyone scrambles to get a room. If you're not quick off the mark, you can end up sharing a double room with up to six people if there is a shortage of accommodation. You wouldn't think it possible, but I've seen it happen. You can be standing around in the foyer for hours, fighting your corner. I'm lucky that my dad will do all that kind of fighting for me and he almost always manages to get me my own room. The way I prepare for fights, I need my own space. It's another one per cent. We try to cover all aspects, and we take this approach whether we're competing in a multi-nations tournament or the Olympic Games.

We have always tried to make sure the environment suits our needs, but sometimes you just have to make do. In London, my apartment was outside the recreational area in the Olympic Village, which was an unfortunate location for us. The first night we stayed, they were practising the music for the opening ceremony right underneath us. The noise outside was deafening. I definitely struggled to adapt to the buzz where we were. I like to have peace and quiet, but what I got was noisy and chaotic. If I'd had a preference I'd have gone where there were fewer people.

My experience and memories of the Olympic Village were mixed. On the one hand, I loved the excitement and enthusiasm in there and the daily routine of crowds and fuss. But on the other hand, I didn't enjoy going into the dining area because there were hundreds of people in there and, in honesty, it was everything I usually avoided when I'm preparing for a bout.

Some people definitely thrived on the buzz and the energy of the place, with all the athletes from all over the world. I admit it was uplifting and fascinating to be a part of an event on such a scale. But I couldn't help feeling that, for what I wanted to achieve from these two weeks in London, there were just too many people enjoying a party atmosphere. With music often blasting away outside, there were times it felt like a rock festival. I remember the first time we walked to the canteen, I turned to Dad and said: 'I don't think some people here realise this is the Olympic Games; they think it's a party.'

I guess everyone prepares in their own way. For some, no doubt, all of this excitement would have helped them to perform at their best. But I'm not like that. I have to have clear separation of things, and in the middle of the most serious competition of my life, I'd consider myself to be anti-social. I didn't like being around the crowds, so instead I used my time focusing on the task ahead and I spent a lot of time on my own in the room reading the scriptures. I became intense during that period, but that's the way I find works best for me when it comes to preparing for action.

Obviously I wouldn't be rude. I talked to the girls in the apartment and I had a great time with them. I'd met Grainne Murphy a couple of times before in Ireland at award ceremonies, so at least there was a familiar face there. And the other girls were very friendly and easy to get along with. Melanie Nocher slipped a lovely card under my door after the final. We hung out a bit more after the competition was over, when I could relax, but during the Olympics we had completely different competition and training schedules, so although we shared the apartment, our paths didn't cross regularly.

> Some people definitely thrived on the buzz and the energy of the place, with all the athletes from all over the world. I admit it was fascinating.

Swimmer Melanie Nocher was just one of those from the Irish team who came to cheer me on during the Olympic final.

In that respect the village was different to the way I normally prepare, which is usually with my dad and family. I might come across as a recluse, and though it may sound strange, in the lead-up to important fights I find that small talk can sap my energy. When I'm with my family, I can sit down and relax and they know what I'm going through; they don't expect me to keep them entertained.

For a lot of people, all they see is me winning championships, and collecting medals or titles, but they don't understand the intensity of the competition. They don't know about the way I have to prepare myself if I want to win. And I always want to win, especially in an event as important as the Olympic Games.

With that in mind, I try to lock myself away from almost everything. Occasionally someone might come in and try to make the mood a little bit more light-hearted for me, thinking I need to relax. There's no doubt that many athletes, including some in my own team, deal with pressure and stress by joking around. They can laugh and chat before fights, and I will often see them jumping around and messing with each other. They have the ability to walk to the ring with a big grin and a wave to the crowd. Nicola Adams, who won the gold medal in London for Great Britain, is a little bit like that, always smiling and joking. Irish silver medallist John Joe Nevin came out smiling and it worked for him too. Paddy Barnes can crack jokes at an important moment, but that's simply part of his personality. For all of those people, that's their way of dealing with the pre-fight nerves.

My way is different and Mam tells me I've always been like that. From the beginning, when I was in boxing exhibitions as a ten-year-old child, I was always serious when it came to competition. It's strange because I'm not at all a serious person outside of sport. Most of my friends would say that I'm very light-hearted. Luckily, they don't know me when I'm competing – I might not have any friends left! It's just my personality. Maybe it is all too intense. But we know now it works for us as a team. I have to take my competition seriously and that affects everything I do before a fight, including how I interact with people.

A few times in the days after the opening ceremony, when we were counting down time to my first bout, I tried to play scrabble with Dad to take our minds off what was going on. I finally said to him, 'I don't even want to think about words.' All I could string together were two-letter words such as 'in' or 'so'. I think my longest word was 'that'.

Even a child could have beaten me – I think Dad believed I was getting punch-drunk, but I just couldn't concentrate on anything other than the fight. I don't think I'm likely to change at this stage – but then why would I?

Dealing with Defeat

It's a serious business. Unfortunately, or fortunately, depending on what way you look at it, I can remember the fights I've lost in more detail than many of the fights I've won. Since my first European Championships as a 17-year-old, I have lost seven times from 139 fights. It is easier for me to remember those defeats. I've learned more as a boxer and more about who I am as a person in those seven losses than I have in the other 132 wins. There were reasons for the losses, and they're important to understand because their influence has helped shape me into the boxer I am now.

The first time I boxed Sofya Ochigava was probably my most disappointing defeat. The fight was in the semi-final of a multi-nations event in Usti in the Czech Republic early in 2010, and afterwards was possibly the lowest point in my career. There was some controversy over the score and my dad was furious at the time, but whatever the score, I know I didn't box well and the loss affected me deeply. It was my first defeat in a few years.

Before that tournament, I had received an invitation to the White House to meet President Barack Obama on St Patrick's Day and was due to travel to Washington soon after I returned from Usti. After the loss, however, I really didn't want to go – I felt unworthy of the invite. After discussing it with my parents, we decided we would go, even if only to spend some time away from training and boxing. Those few days I spent in Washington really changed something in me. I spent the time reflecting on the loss and immersing myself in scriptures trying to remind myself of every promise God had ever given me. I came away from that trip with a deep conviction that God had great plans for me and that I would get a chance to redeem what had happened in Usti. The next time I faced Ochigava, in the European final in Rotterdam, those convictions mattered, what had happened in the past didn't matter and I knew that final belonged to me.

There have been times where I have also been at the bad end of a decision and I've learned things from those defeats, too. When I boxed against a Bulgarian, Denitsa Eliseeva, in Bulgaria in 2011 in another multi-nations tournament, there was no doubt in my mind that I had clearly won the fight. In the ring, the referee even raised my hand as the winner. Then a competition official announced that the other girl had won. Eliseeva is such an honourable boxer that she came over to me and apologised for the decision.

She was aware of what happened. After that I think the whole Bulgarian federation was suspended. It wasn't me alone who fell foul to a political decision in that tournament, as Britain's Nicola Adams did too. The trade paper *Boxing News* wrote about it and commented that the Adams fight was robbery, but that the one involving me was the worst decision they had ever seen in amateur boxing.

What I learned from that bout was that I was giving the judges some room to allow them to press their scoring buttons for my opponent. I was staying too long after I scored a punch against Eliseeva. Even though I wasn't being hit, if she threw out her hands and I was in range, the judges were scoring points for her. I needed to get in and out before a signal had even been sent from her brain to her hand telling her to punch. I had to make sure I did not give the judges any opportunity to press for the other girl.

> There have been times where I have also been at the bad end of a decision and I've learned things from those defeats, too.

> *Although I'm not really a star-spotter, I have to admit there was one person I really did hope to see around the village: Roger Federer.*

In training after that I began to work intensively on my legs: in and out, in and out. All the focus was on my legs. At the time in Bulgaria, I was so angry at the injustice of the decision because these types of bad decisions are the things that make people leave amateur boxing and try other sports. After a few weeks, I forgot about it and was able to take the positive from it, and it gave me something new to work on in the gym.

Mam remembers the first time I ever lost. It happened in Riccione, Italy, when I was up against the Russian Yuliya Nemtsova in my debut European Championships in 2004. That time, I went out of the competition on the first day so we had to wait around the whole week until the tournament was over. Our flights back to Ireland were booked for after the finals. I was devastated, I think I spent the remainder of the week crying in my room. Seeing the state I was in, the question my mam asked me was whether I wanted to continue doing this. She asked if I would rather have come to Italy and experienced the loss or stayed at home in Ireland and not bothered. I knew that I had wanted to go to Italy, but I also knew I didn't want to feel like this again.

Losing fights like that can be character-building; it is all part of the journey. It's easy to live life on the mountain-top. It's when you are down in the valley and you have to get back up that's hard. That's where you have to grow as a person. If you ask me, it's there that a true champion is born.

Living in the Olympic Village was another minor obstacle we had to climb to reach our mountain-top of Olympic glory, so Dad and I did what we always try to do, which was to get a routine going. Even visiting the canteen for food, we had a set plan. We'd go in and walk round to the right-hand side of the room, where there was usually nobody sitting. I went to get the pasta. Dad went to get the chicken. Teamwork. I stuck to the same simple food throughout my entire time there, except on the days of the fights when my stomach closes up with nervous tension.

Occasionally, on a day I wasn't fighting or after a fight, I did break the routine, and went out to eat in the nearby Westfield Shopping Centre so I could meet up with the rest of my family. There was a Jamie Oliver restaurant there, which was where we tended to go. Going there helped to break up the day for us, as time can pass slowly when you are cooped up in the village. So I would sit there for a couple of hours with my family and watch the people go by.

I'm often asked what it was like in the Olympic Village, where there were so many world-famous athletes milling around. I remember on my first visit to the athletes' canteen I saw Usain Bolt. We were walking in as the great Jamaican was coming out, and that was our glancing contact with the world's fastest man. He was the first well-known athlete we saw in the Olympic Village!

On another day when we arrived for our meal, we noticed loads of security outside the canteen and a shiny Rolls Royce parked where there wasn't a parking space. The Queen was coming out of a building from across the road. I don't usually get that excited about those sorts of things, and I never bring a camera with me, but I did give her a wave and I'm convinced she waved back to me.

Although I'm not really a star-spotter, I have to admit there was one person I really did hope to see around the village: tennis star Roger Federer. I'm a huge fan of his. Sadly, I never saw him and, although I like to keep myself to myself, if I had spotted him, I would have definitely jumped at the opportunity to introduce myself. But I knew it wasn't about who I could meet. I was there on business, and that meant preparing for either Natasha Jonas or Queen Underwood, one of whom was due to be my first opponent.

CHAPTER 5

THE ROAD
TO THE FINAL

This is it. I am finally boxing in the Olympic Games.

Escaping the Crowds

As far as the Irish fans were concerned, my first Olympic fight was a brave new world. Although I tried to shut myself away from all the distractions as I prepared for it, the stories of London turning green were filtering back to me via the Irish team and their families. The message was that it was on an entirely different scale from anything we might have expected.

In the Olympic Village, however, I didn't fully realise what was going on. But Mam and my sister Sarah were staying in a part of London far from the boxing venue, and they had to travel across the city to come to watch me. Their trek to the ExCeL Arena opened their eyes.

On their journey to the Docklands, Mam told Sarah that she was feeling nervous, because she was worried that their support, and any other Irish people who had got in to the arena, would be drowned out by the noise that the home fans were making. For, as Dad and I had expected, Natasha Jonas had beaten Queen Underwood the day before, by 21-13, and the Liverpool-born boxer was sure to get terrific backing from the crowd. The support among the British public for their athletes in the Olympics was amazing and they were doing a

(*Previous page*) Entering the ExCeL Arena ahead of my quarter-final bout against Team GB's Natasha Jonas.

great job in rallying the troops. We expected they would raise the roof to cheer on Jonas.

However, even when they were on the tube, Mam was aware that things might be very different. She pointed out to Sarah: 'There's an awful lot of Irish people on this train.' When they reached the ExCeL, all the Irish piled off the carriages at the same time. Mam and Sarah had to walk over a footbridge across one of the Thames docks and then came down some steep steps at the other side to get to the main entrance of the arena.

Because they were early, they decided to sit around outside and wait, watching as the trains on the Docklands Light Rail arrived every two minutes. As each one let out its passengers, the fans flooded down the steps towards the boxing venue. Mam kept looking at Sarah as if to say: 'Are you thinking what I'm thinking?' The Irish were descending on the place in their thousands.

They saw guys wearing 'onesies', ridiculous giant, green, one-piece pyjama suits, with their faces painted green and orange. Gangs of girls from Cork, Wicklow and Dublin marched arm in arm, with tricolours painted on their faces, as they headed towards what for many was their first boxing match. There were whole families with their flags, their false red beards and wide brim straw hats. There was no missing the fact that the Irish had arrived, and Mam and Sarah thought it was lovely to see.

They were pouring in from all corners of Ireland, from all parishes and all sporting backgrounds, bringing their football and their GAA into a hall in London to shout for an Irish boxer against Natasha Jonas, the great British hope. Although the Irish seemed to be everywhere, Mam also noticed the Chinese, the Turks, the Russians and the Japanese – people of every race all coming together to celebrate a great sporting occasion.

> There was no missing the fact that the Irish had arrived, and Mam and Sarah thought it was lovely to see.

Two girls and a teenage boy walked past dressed in togas. It turned out they were on their way to the Greco-Roman wrestling, which was also being staged at the ExCeL Olympic site. There were other sports, too: table tennis, judo, weightlifting and fencing all took place there, and some 70,000 people (almost the capacity of the Olympic Stadium) passed through the venue most days.

Who could have predicted that so many people would travel over from Ireland to see me fight, or that the Irish would outnumber the British supporters by five to one.

We knew the Olympics would be big, and that there would be a huge crowd, which was why we'd prepared for it with my fight at the Dublin O2 back in 2009, but even so we weren't expecting this. Who could have predicted that so many people would travel over from Ireland to see me fight, or that the Irish would outnumber the British supporters by five to one and create such an incredible atmosphere? You couldn't buy it. Irish people were coming in from everywhere, including the cable cars that were running from the London Dome across to the street directly in front of the ExCeL, all with their mad hats and their tee-shirts and flags.

Mam's sister Yvonne lives in London and she also came down with some of her family for the bout. They all kept gaping in amazement at these mobs of Irish fans, wondering what was going on. For London and boxing, it was unusual. People didn't normally come to competitions in those numbers. But this was the Olympics.

I'd heard from some of the lads in the Irish boxing team, who had started their campaigns before me, about how they had received great support. It was good to hear, but I couldn't allow myself to get caught up in the atmosphere and the expectation of it all.

So I didn't get distracted. I tried to remove myself from it all, and to help with that I even turned off my phone a week before the Olympics started. I had been getting texts from lots of people,

Just some of the Irish fans arriving at the ExCeL Arena – the support I received was astonishing.

> Having won the World Championship title earlier in the year I was given a bye in the first round, but after that it got more difficult.

and I didn't want to read them then. I really couldn't afford to be interested in what was happening in the rest of the world. Coming up to what I knew was going to be the fight of my life so far, I deliberately locked myself away from the outside world. I just kept a phone that only my family knew the number for, so that I could keep in touch with them. Otherwise, no one could speak to me.

Natasha Jonas

As soon as the original draw for the Olympics had been made, some people had commented that my half of it was definitely the tougher one, with a likely run of difficult bouts up to the final. I was the top seed, having won the World Championship title earlier in the year, and because of this I was given a bye in the first round, but after that it got more difficult.

I would face either Jonas or Queen Underwood in my first fight. After Jonas won, Dad knew that if I beat her I would meet the winner of the bout between Mavzuna Chorieva and Cheng Dong in the semi-final. If I won that contest, Dad expected me to meet the number two seed Sofya Ochigava in the final. They were all going to be challenging fights.

Dad pointed out that, even though all the top seeded girls were in my end of the draw, it was tougher for them to fight against me. There is no sense worrying about the draw, as it is out of my control, so I try to be prepared for anyone. We also decided that the draw was perfect for me, because I'd said that I wanted to box against the best in the competition and I have never shied away from it. If I faced the best in the world it was going to be difficult, but it would also lift me and help me to get more out of myself.

Despite that ambition to fight the better girls and showcase boxing on the biggest stage it has ever been on, I wasn't complacent about the task, despite my number one seeding. We had it set in our heads that Jonas would beat Underwood, which would set up the perfect match between Ireland and England. Jonas was fine for me. It's not that normal, but I love to box against the home girl.

No matter where the competition is, the atmosphere in the arena when the home girl is involved is different. I boxed against Cheng Dong in the 2008 World Championship final in China and the atmosphere was buzzing and loud. I expected that in London, when I went in against Jonas, the mood of the crowd would be even more intense and noisy than it had been then, because the Olympics were sure to make it an extra-special occasion.

Liverpool's Natasha Jonas (blue) lands a punch against Queen Underwood on her way to a 21-13 victory to set up a quarter-final bout with me.

Fully focused on the task ahead before the Natasha Jonas fight.

All through the day, Monday 6 August, my feelings were a mix of nerves and anticipation of getting started. It wasn't until I was in the locker room getting changed into my gear that I finally began to take in the enormity of what I was doing. I was holding myself together well, but quietly thinking: 'This is it. This is it. I am finally boxing in the Olympic Games and pulling the Irish vest with Team Ireland on it over my head.'

I remember each moment of getting ready: seeing the vest beside me on the bench, holding the vest in my hands, and then putting on the vest. They were the personal moments that were beginning to get to me. Little things I had often imagined were now suddenly real, and it was a revelation. The act of dressing in the singlet of my country was spine-tingling. I was now living the dream I had as a child.

Everything about putting on the Irish Olympic team uniform was a beautiful, simple pleasure – the small crest on the singlet, the shorts, even the colours and the material – those basic things were just incredible. I was sitting in the changing room saying to myself: this is the dream. Not for the first time, I realised what a privilege it was for me to be in this position.

I was not overly concerned about drawing Jonas, but I was aware that I tend to worry about the first fight in any competition, let alone the Olympic Games. The first contest has always been the most difficult for me, as I can sometimes be a slow starter in the opening bouts. I usually need at least one fight to get myself into the swing of things, and that thought was swirling around in my head because, world champion or not, the last thing I could afford was to have a bad day or to be lax against a girl of Jonas's calibre. I needed to be at the top of my form or I wouldn't win.

> It wasn't until I was in the locker room getting changed into my gear that I finally began to take in the enormity of what I was doing.

> The truth of the matter is that I don't study the draw when I go into a tournament, so my mind wasn't on who I would meet later on.

It was something that I was aware of throughout the week, even though I had previously beaten her 6-3 in the semi-final of the 2011 Strandja Memorial tournament in Pazardjic, Bulgaria. Since that time, however, they had changed the scoring patterns, and the scores in fights were much lower then than they are today. Dad's view was that under the old system it seemed as though one had to almost knock out an opponent to get a point from the judges; now they are much more generous with the scoring.

Dad believed that Natasha Jonas was the most improved boxer in the world in my weight division, under 60 kilograms, and that she would provide a tough challenge for my first bout. Of course, he told me that only afterwards, what he actually said to me before the fight was that she was the one fighter that he wanted me to get.

In most big tournaments, we know that there will be four hard rounds at every stage and in that case it was going to be a battle regardless of which girl came through. I had fought them both before and I knew their abilities, but I took comfort from having had tricky first fights early in competitions before, against tough Turkish girls and Chinese girls, and I've always been able to produce.

I take the view that each fight is going to be different. The first time we shared the ring in Bulgaria, Jonas showed me a lot of respect and, rather than open up with all her artillery, she stayed covered up. Dad suspected that her tactics would change for this fight and thought she would try to throw everything at me this time round. What we saw from her in her fight against Underwood did nothing to change our minds. Dad is so good at reading how fights will go – I remember him saying on television that he thought Jonas would beat Underwood by seven or eight points and she ended up winning 21-13.

The reason we didn't read too much into the fight between Jonas and Underwood was that the American has a completely different style of boxing to me. In her bout, Jonas was trying to keep her distance from Underwood, and when she got the lead she made sure she kept away from her. The first round is almost always critical in these fights, as very few people are able to come back from being behind and win. To be truthful, this went pretty much as we had expected, even if we had to recognise that she was a much-improved fighter from the one I'd met the year before.

Into the Ring

While we had predicted most things until now, the never-to-be-forgotten atmosphere in my quarter-final bout took us completely by surprise. I know I had tried to prepare for it with the real eye opener at the Bernard Dunne world title fight in Dublin in 2009, but no one could have adequately predicted the frenzy I faced when I went into the ring with Jonas. It was like feeding time at the zoo: it seemed as though everybody was rattling their cages and making as much noise as they could.

The Irish fans erupted the first time they caught a glimpse of me in my gear as I went to get my bandages stamped. But even before that, I could hear people chanting my name and stamping as I readied myself for the fight. I don't think the officials fully understood what was happening, because they had never seen anything like it at an amateur boxing tournament before. I had barely taken a few steps into the auditorium when the crowd exploded into life and while I wasn't to know at that point, it would soon become a familiar experience the whole way through the week.

The fight itself was cracking – the best I've been involved in for a long time and a real hurricane of a contest, even if there was a small blip for me in the second round.

The first two minutes went as well as I could have hoped for. I had my range and timing and I ended it 5-2 ahead. I was moving well; I felt comfortable and aware. I could tell I was ahead before I even walked over to Dad and Zauri in the corner, because the crowd was going berserk when the scores flashed up on the big screens. I couldn't see the scores between rounds, because the screens were facing away from the ring, but the fans could see all five judges' marks and that I was three points ahead.

At the start of the second round, I remember Jonas caught me with a few scoring shots and I was finding it difficult to time my shots at her. That's when I heard Dad screaming at me: 'You have to be first against her.' By this he meant that I should attack her before she found the opportunity to attack me. It was at that point I started making my attacks more frequent, because Dad was right – I had been waiting for her a bit too much at the start of the second round and I was getting caught.

Sometimes even when I understand what I need to do, it takes time to adjust and be effective, but in the second minute of the second round I was beginning to get my attacking moves landing more efficiently and started to build my points back up again. I ended the round keeping the three-point lead and again the crowd told me the good news when the bell sounded with the score at 10-7.

It was a good end to what was a poor start to the round and definitely a rough patch for me. It was also frustrating, because Dad had his head under the ropes and was screaming at me, but I couldn't hear what he was saying. Normally, I can pick his voice out from everything else, but with the constant wall of noise in the arena even my tuned-in ears were failing. After the fight we found out why I had difficulty as the noise, recorded at 114 decibels, actually broke the

Olympic record and was close to the noise of a jumbo jet taking off. I'd never experienced support like it.

To be three points ahead was encouraging, but I went into the third round needing to be more aggressive for the second half of the fight, because I'm best when I let my combinations go off in fast three- or four-punch attacks. That was the key to winning the bout.

My speed and footwork have always been huge factors for me in everything I do, whether it is football, GAA or boxing, and when I am able to let my combinations go off in those quick attacking moves, or when I am feinting well, and all these different things come together, I am able to make it difficult for anyone to beat me. I knew that although this was my first fight of the competition,

After an even second round, I took charge in the third.

> I knew that although this was my first fight of the competition, it was going to put one of us on the Olympic podium and earn a bronze medal for either Bray or Liverpool.

it was going to put one of us on the Olympic podium and earn a bronze medal for either Bray or Liverpool.

With Jonas trailing, in the third round she came out like a bull in a china shop and it was up to me not just to weather the storm but to use her desperation to my own advantage. I was comfortably able to handle her aggression and was scoring well myself. I knew I had a good lead when the bell sounded, not least because the crowd once again let me know. In fact, I had won the round 9-4 and now led by 19-11.

It was such a big lead that for the final two-minute round, all I had to think about was to make no slip-ups, stay in control and continue scoring. I was still landing scores and was able to give her a second standing count in the final round. The end result was never in doubt: I won with a decent 11-point margin, 26-15.

Everything had worked out wonderfully and I was happy with my fight performance, although afterwards the perfectionist in me could see things I didn't do well. But those quibbles could wait as I felt relief at getting through and some of the pressure began to lift.

The Team United

I had negotiated the first fight comfortably and the crowd were letting me know all about it – it was a wonderful moment. As the referee was raising my hand, I looked up and saw my Irish team-mates Adam Nolan and flyweight Michael Conlan in the stands shouting down to me and pumping the air. Delighted for me, I could see the emotion written all over their faces. They had been telling me that before my fights they can hardly talk, because they are feeling nervous for me and feeling the pressure. In honesty, they are like extended family and are constantly looking out for me. The team spirit we have is something special.

In training camps I often feel the same support, because I'm the only woman among all of the lads and it is natural that they are protective towards me. Even during the Games, we were seeing each other in the athletes' village each day because I'd be training with them. I think it pulled us all together and we remained a close-knit group for the entire competition.

The fact that they continued to support me and the rest of the team was particularly hard for Adam and Darren O'Neill, as they had both been knocked out of the tournament before I had my first fight. Although they were disappointed, they both took the attitude that they were going to hang in with the team and that's what they did. Darren was a brilliant, faithful captain in London, and when he lost his fight in the last 16, he and Adam redirected all of their energy into supporting us. They were always sitting up in the stands in their green tracksuits waving and screaming at the ring. I don't think many athletes would have been capable of doing that after such crushing disappointment and it couldn't have been easy.

It wasn't their only show of loyalty. Later in the tournament, when Darren's room-mate John Joe Nevin lost his bantamweight final 14-11 to Britain's Luke Campbell, Darren was crying. When you spend so much intense time together, and train and spar hard as a squad, you build up a closeness between you all. I suppose that carried through, hoping that everyone performed well, but in the competitive environment of an Olympic Games you have your own stuff to deal with and you have to let others' disappointments go. You can't let it affect you. Darren and Adam, more than anyone else, knew that I couldn't let their defeats interfere with what I was trying to do.

Amazing Support

Team captain Darren O'Neill (centre) watching from the stands with Dad and Adam Nolan.

It was only as I left the ring that I was able for the first time to really enjoy the mood and energy of the stadium. The support was a powerful shot in the arm, but it was uncharacteristic for me to be so emotional when I was still involved in a competition. I'd never seen so many happy people and, just as Mam had seen them flood down the steps when

she waited to come in, here they were in front of me, Irish flags everywhere, men, women and kids – all of them pumped.

I could see for the first time the breadth of the support I had, because I had the blinkers on before the fight and had to focus on the bout when I was coming into the ring. But when it was announced that I had won, I looked up and tried to take in all the craziness.

People often ask me: do the crowd make any difference when you are in the middle of a fight? The answer is yes, and that day against Jonas I was lifted.

People often ask me: do the crowd make any difference when you are in the middle of a fight? The answer is yes, and that day against Jonas I was lifted. During the second round when I had the blip, the crowd definitely had an input and they were able to help me get myself back up again. I also saw it with some of the British boxers – when they fell behind in a few matches, they were able to come back. Normally, you very rarely see that in amateur boxing, but in the ExCeL the crowd often carried their fighter along with them.

Every little bit helped, and my brother Peter was in the crowd stressing over every move. The daughter of Des Donnelly, the Irish team manager, was sitting a few seats in front of Peter and took a great photograph of him; he is sitting there like a wreck with his hands covering his head. That was what I was putting my family through! He couldn't watch and spent the entire time coming in and out of the stadium every few minutes.

Afterwards he said to me: 'Every time I came back in, you were giving the girl a standing count.' I replied: 'In that case you should have gone out more often.' My family always find it hard to watch my fights, but because it was the Olympic Games they all knew how much it meant. When I won, I think they were all roaring crying.

For an hour or so, I was able to enjoy the fact that I was guaranteed at least a bronze medal, but very quickly began to get nervous about

With my niece Madeleine, who was probably my youngest supporter in London.

the next fight against Tajikistan's Mavzuna Chorieva, who I knew was waiting for me in the semi-final. However, for that brief period of down time, I headed back with my family towards the Olympic Park and into the Westfield shopping centre in Stratford. I knew I had a rest day the next day, and so there was no urgency for me to start preparing for Chorieva immediately.

I was able to spend some time with my family; we even had a meal there, with no Irish people round at all. I'd say they were all still at the ExCeL singing. Peter was there with his wife Kim and their baby girl Madeleine; my sister Sarah was there too. I also had some lovely texts from my eldest brother Lee who was travelling over the next day with his partner Nicola and their sons Jason and Aaron. Everyone was excited. 'I can't believe my sister is an Olympic medallist,' Sarah was saying. I loved being round them, because they made me feel brilliant about myself.

Mam told me how proud she was of what I'd done. Sarah admitted that when she was walking with the crowds before we met, all she wanted to say was: 'Do you know who my sister is?' She wanted to tell everybody about my medal, and what I had done. When I look back on the Olympics, those were some of the best moments for me. To see my three-month-old niece Madeleine with her tiny Irish tee-shirt was a perfect close to the evening. They are the small things that help to give you a break from the intensity of competition, and in this instance my permanent smile became a good deal bigger. Everyone was buzzing about the fact we were on the podium now. But if anyone knew me like my family did, they knew bronze was never going to be the colour of the medal I wanted.

> If anyone knew me like my family did, they knew bronze was never going to be the colour of the medal I wanted.

Showboating Tajik Style

I knew Mavzuna Chorieva pretty well by this stage of my career. I had fought her in the semi-finals of the World Championships in China earlier in the year and won 16-6. We had gone into that bout expecting to face her getting up to some of her usual antics in the ring. Dad had prepared me for more of the same this time round, saying she was going to do quite a lot of showboating in the ring. He told me to expect that she would put out her tongue and stick her chin out at me. She had done a bit of it in China too, but clowning like that doesn't affect me in any way. I would be more practical and think about where I was going to get my next point from. I'd focus on winning the fight more than wondering about her dancing around.

Although she does joke around, I wasn't blind to the fact that Chorieva is also a very talented boxer. She is still young, just 19 years old then, so I feel that she is going to get better and better. I expect to see a lot more of her in the coming years, but in London I knew that she was definitely a dangerous opponent. She has the sort of physique that suggests she is going to be a real fighter, but in the ring she is actually an effective counter-puncher. She is very, very fast, so I had to think hard about how I was going to fight against her and be clever about it.

I knew I would have to throw in plenty of feints against her and try to make her think I was going to attack one way and then attack a different way. Above all, I needed to be patient. Against a boxer like her, I had to choose carefully how I scored points, and I couldn't afford to be impulsive.

I recognised that the showboating thing was about her trying to distract me. The reason boxers such as Chorieva do this is they are hoping to annoy their opponents to the point where they lose patience

The podium in China: Sofya Ochigava, me, Mavzuna Chorieva and Natasha Jonas. Little did I know I would have to beat them all to win Olympic gold.

and try to go in when they shouldn't, or else try to land a certain type of punch that they have no business trying to land. If I'd got sucked in in that way, she would have been able to pick up points and score off her opponent's impatience and lack of discipline. That was the idea behind her dancing routine and sticking out her tongue. Sofya Ochigava occasionally does something similar, too, so I really needed to keep my mind sharp and in the right place.

The Semi-final

The jab is the most important punch for any boxer, not just me. All the great boxers have a strong jab.

Dad said to be patient and I was patient against Chorieva. When I saw she wanted me to come in to her so she could counter-punch and start scoring, I wasn't tempted. I kept focusing on doing my own thing, working on getting the next score, and trying not to get caught myself. Of course that is something I suppose I always try to do – I hate giving up silly points or being hit by stupid shots that I should have avoided.

But I was keeping my left hand busy and using plenty of feints. The jab is the most important punch for any boxer, not just me. All the great boxers have a strong jab. It sets up everything else, so I had to keep my jab busy all the time. In the first 30 seconds of a fight in particular, I make sure my left hand is constantly busy, because that is the time when I'm trying to work out my opponent and determine what's going to happen in the rest of the bout.

The opening exchanges are also when I am trying to get my timing and my distance right. In the first phase of most fights, there is always a sequence of feints and both boxers tend to do a lot of probing. My fight against Chorieva followed this pattern, and my jab was extremely busy.

I went into the fight still feeling fresh after beating Jonas. Contrary to what people may have thought, I was suffering no physical issues at all after my first bout. I know it looked like Jonas was hitting me with everything, including that famous kitchen sink, which she said after the fight she had thrown at me, but my body was in good condition. There was no tiredness or soreness, and I had stuck to my strict routine of having a rub down and putting plenty of fluids back into my system to make sure I felt my best.

(*Overleaf*) Mavzuna Chorieva and I warily look for an opening during our semi-final bout.

This time the crowd didn't seem quite as mad as it was against Jonas, but despite that we were far from complacent.

Because we knew what to expect from her, it didn't mean that the fight was going to be straightforward. This time the crowd didn't seem quite as mad as it was against Jonas, but despite that we were far from complacent. After all, this was a fight for a place in the first-ever women's lightweight Olympic final. We both knew that world champions sometimes fall when it comes to the Olympic Games, and that there were different pressures and a different atmosphere to that in the regular competitions at European and world level, so I approached Chorieva cautiously.

Chorieva feels the full force of my right glove during our Olympic contest.

Dad and I agreed that I should go into the ring with the view of allowing her to come to me in the first instance, and that when I decided the time was right to attack her, it was crucial for me to get close beforehand. If I couldn't do that, she was going to pick me off. At times during the bout, I also edged her on to the ropes, which was good because it meant she couldn't back away and I could gain some points. As the fight continued, I was generally able to box my own fight, staying clever about my decisions and keeping thinking in the ring.

Dad told me what combinations to be aware of and what punches she regularly threw. He also explained how the fight would unfold and predicted that she would do the wobbly leg showboating and dancing and she would stick out her chin. I watched her and made sure I didn't dive in, but I knew that if Chorieva stuck her head out at me and the shot was on, I would hit her.

Again, just as it was with Jonas, I knew after each round by the crowd's reaction to the scoreboard whether they were happy or not and how I had done by the judges. I felt the same way as I did in the first fight and didn't want to get drawn into the emotion of the fans. I had to be so disciplined about that aspect, because it could have cost me so much. Against effective counter-punchers like her, if you give points away, you have to go and chase after them, which is exactly what they want you to do, so the game-plan has to be more set.

Against Jonas, who boxes like a real fighter, I could express myself much more and really let my combinations go. I could box against her and fight against her and I could mix it up, but that was definitely not the case against Chorieva. She was content to go through the eight minutes without making any significant attacks, even though she was down in every round.

To describe it as a straightforward win would be to over-simplify the 17-9 score, because it was all about the pace and timing. My approach

It was all working nicely
for me, so I was able to
stay in control and I didn't
hit any speed bumps in
any of the four rounds.

was one, two, three and get out of there. It was all working nicely for me, so I was able to stay in control and I didn't hit any speed bumps in any of the four rounds.

In the first two minutes, she didn't throw many punches but decided on theatrics rather than tactics. She wasn't able to score off me, and I was 3-1 ahead after that. I felt that my footwork was good and I was landing clean shots. After the second round, at 7-3 ahead, I felt I was heading towards an uncomplicated victory. Dad and Zauri were pleased, but they didn't need to remind me that going two points or four points up is not a big margin, so I kept vigilant and aware throughout. In the end I was able to cruise into the Olympic final.

If people look back, I hope they will see that my bout with Jonas was one of the best of the entire competition. The final was obviously the most important, but many have said to me since then that the Jonas fight had the 'wow' factor about it that very few other fights had. It takes two opponents to make a fight rise above the rest, and I thought the tempo and intensity of that bout opened people's eyes to women's boxing. *Boxing News* magazine said it was the fight of the championship, which sent out an important message that women's boxing had arrived.

Dad has said that the reason he believes it had such an impact was the shock factor; it jolted everyone who saw it because it was so ferocious and aggressive. When he looks back at my three fights, he believes that Jonas really came to win, while Chorieva and Ochigava came into the ring aiming not to lose. It was Natasha's approach that shocked people and that's what made it such a compelling spectacle to watch.

Having just earned a gold-medal fight to keep my dream alive, I had to focus immediately on the task ahead. This time there was no chance to see my family after I'd beaten Chorieva. I was scheduled to box the next day against Ochigava, and I wanted to continue the business and get back to the Olympic Village for my rub down from physiotherapist Connor McCarthy. After that, once again I went for a walk with Dad up through Olympic Park and over to the boulevards beside the main stadium. For the first time in my life, I had an Olympic final to talk to him about.

I salute the fans at the ExCeL Arena, but already my mind was turning to the final.

E FINAL:
SS GAMES AND
CKEN NUGGETS

I wasn't scared by the situation. I knew exactly what I had to do.

Preparing for the Final

In the end it came down to two rounds. Over the next five minutes, I would either become an Olympic champion or I would lose in a major final for the first time in seven years. Sport has a habit of presenting things in bleak terms and for me the options were either failure or the fulfilling of a dream, there was nothing in between.

It was the biggest fight of my life and moments from the past stacked up in front of me. But the image that remained closest to me was the ten-year-old daddy's girl and the Olympic seed planted in my heart 16 years before. More than ever before, I had to believe that that seed was God-given, that it was my destiny. How could I believe anything else, since this dream had remained with me all these years from childhood until now, without ever fading. From an early age, I knew I was different; I wasn't like other girls. That fact was brought home to me by having to pretend I was a boy so I could fight. Sometimes, it was only when I took off my headgear at the end of the fight that they realised I was a girl.

As I got older, boys were increasingly reluctant to spar or fight against me, because they were afraid of being beaten and that they might lose face with their friends. I can understand the dilemma from their perspective, but at the time it made it near impossible for my dad to get me fights, and I was incredibly frustrated that I wasn't getting the same opportunities that the lads I trained with were getting, or that my brothers were getting.

It wasn't until I was 15 that I was eventually able to box Belfast's Alana Murphy in the first female fight to be officially sanctioned in Ireland, a bout that took place on Halloween 2001. Before that, women's boxing didn't exist in any official capacity in this country and any exhibitions or fights I had previously fought against the lads were against the regulations. That historic fight was a spring-board for me and for Irish female boxing, and over the next couple of years, I would gain more experience as women's boxing became increasingly accepted.

Now, with my lifetime ambition hanging in the balance, the choice was a cruel, imperfect finish or the Olympic climax I longed for. I knew that the final against Sofya Ochigava would be a tech-nical affair, they always are, and for the long hours beforehand it was impossible to relax with the pressure bearing down. My stomach was churning.

I was trying to approach the Olympic final like any other fight, but no matter how much I tried to convince myself that this was just another fight, I knew that it wasn't, I knew that this was more than just a fight. I wasn't worried about my capacity to win: I was confident and I believed that I had the ability to beat the Russian, but the struggle that day was controlling the nerves. I know I couldn't have handled it alone, not without prayer.

I had boxed Ochigava three times in the past and the record was 2-1 in my favour, but that was irrelevant to the here and now. If previous results had any bearing, it was the fact that we knew each other too well in the ring, and the fight would be most likely even more tentative than usual. I knew the fight was going to be close,

> We were pretty certain that it was going to be a cagey fight, and that she wouldn't come out blazing or throw caution to the wind.

so I had to prepare myself for a disciplined fight that could go right down to the last punch. I also had to focus on the tactics that Dad had devised after long and hard planning. My job was to execute that plan, despite the pressure and regardless of the nerves.

The last time I met her was earlier in the year in China in the final of the World Championships. We had no reason to expect anything but a similar, cautious style from her this time round. We were pretty certain that it was going to be a cagey fight, and that she wouldn't come out blazing or throw caution to the wind. Ochigava is a wily and very clever boxer and, with the quality of their team and the coaches at her disposal in Russia, I was fully expecting the toughest fight of my life.

The constant about Ochigava was that I had never seen her boxing any differently from the technical counter-punching style she normally adopts. In all the years I'd known her, I had never seen her fighting aggressively. She had never come out like Natasha Jonas did against me in the first round of our quarter-final bout.

I knew I was the more versatile boxer, I can be aggressive if I need to be, in fact, Ochigava would have loved for me to have come out like that and to have taken the fight to her. She would have liked to see me come out and box the way I had to box to beat Natasha Jonas: aggressively pushing forward with my attacks. If I did that, we would have been fighting the fight she wanted. The world number two is more comfortable on the back foot picking off her opponents with expertly chosen counter-attacks. And once she had the lead, she would have spent the rest of the fight keeping her distance – that is the way that counter-punchers think and box.

Because our past meetings had been close-fought encounters, this suggested that if either of us had a bad day we would almost certainly lose the final, and I suppose that thought was constantly trying to break into my mind. I had to counter any doubt with a scripture, you can't let these little doubts grow into big fears. It was no surprise that we were meeting to decide who should take home the gold medal: we were definitely the top two boxers in the lightweight division. In my mind, there wasn't anyone else in the Olympic competition that could have beaten Ochigava.

Generally, just one or two points decide titles in meetings like these, but I don't think the fight unfolded in a way people would have expected. Beforehand, analysts were saying on television and in the newspapers that whoever took the early lead was probably going to win the gold medal. That sounded like a fairly sensible prediction; after all, we were both excellent counter-punchers so it would seem near impossible to pull back a lead against the other. Dad had a different opinion, he was completely confident that if I went behind, I had the ability to change my tactics and pull the fight back in my favour.

On the other hand, if Ochigava fell behind, it was going to be more difficult for her to pull it back, because she is an out-and-out counter-puncher and she finds it hard to come forward and be the offensive boxer. She could come forward on her terms and at her pace, but if she was forced into boxing on the front foot, she'd be boxing outside her comfort zone.

I knew clearly what I had to do against her and recognised that each round would be close, with marginal advantages taken by one fighter or the other. Short of a catastrophic error by one of us, neither boxer was going to run away with the fight and rack up a huge score. It just wasn't going to happen. What was vital was to stay calm and composed throughout. At the time, I didn't realise how important that sort of thinking would be in the end, or how vital it was in the first few moments of the final.

My chance to fulfil my dream: climbing into the ring at the start of the Olympic final.

The Final Begins

It must have been for less than half a minute, but when the bell sounded for the start of the fight, although I was bouncing around and seemed to be moving well, I couldn't get going. I could see every punch that was coming, but I didn't seem to be able to react to them in the way that I usually could. I had to step back and clear out of Ochigava's way to stop her from scoring. Meanwhile, I almost had to force my left hand to leave my face in order to get my jab going.

It seemed as though I was going through the motion of pushing out the shots, but there was a resistance. That first part of the fight seemed endless, but in real time it was no longer than the opening moments. This had never happened before. It was like there was a weight bearing down on my shoulders and my head was cloudy. I couldn't concentrate on what I needed to do. I'm not sure if it was simply the pressure of the occasion or something deeper, but either way I thank God it lifted and my punches started to flow.

After the two minutes of the first round had come to a close, I was content to get back to my corner to see Dad and coach Zauri Antia.

I felt the round had gone well despite the concerns of the opening moments. I thought I might have been a point up but the score was level at 2-2, and I was satisfied with that. With that round behind me, I felt a lot more relaxed and happier than I was in the first 20 seconds.

It's amazing how moods can shift in a fight; within seconds you can go from being in an uncomfortable struggle to being in charge and confident. That was what happened here, because by the break I really did feel sharper. Dad was saying to me: 'Everything is great, everything is going well. Keep doing what you're doing and continue to be patient.' He also added: 'Try to get a little bit closer to her before you start your attack, sometimes you're too far out.'

> It's amazing how moods can shift; within seconds you can go from being in a struggle to being in charge.

Sofya Ochigava lands a rare punch during our cautious bout.

The scoreboard shows that I am a point behind after two rounds, but I remained calm.

Round Two

For a lot of the time in the second round I was feinting – trying to make her react with some punches so that I could then counter-punch her. It was tit-for-tat all of the time, a thinking match where we were both inviting the other to throw the first punch so that we could score with our own counter-attacks. Like all of our fights before, it was again turning into a game of chess more than a punching brawl. We were circling the ring and watching each other, both of us waiting for the other to do something, to show their hand. There would be a flurry of activity as we both tried to snatch some scores and then it was back to the tense game of chess.

In retrospect, I was a bit too passive in round two and I paid the price; the score after the round was 4-3 to Ochigava. To the pundits, this was the nightmare situation for me: to be behind against the girl widely regarded as the best out-and-out counter-puncher in the world wasn't exactly ideal. But I wasn't scared by the situation. I knew exactly what I had to do as I came back to my corner for a second time. I believed my Dad when he told me I could pull back the lead from her.

I just had to execute Dad's tactics better. Honestly, at this stage, I was still very confident; I was a point down, but we were composed.

I think that a few years ago, when I was in my early twenties, I might have become uptight about it and started to worry more about the clock ticking down. With my experience, I knew that trailing by one point or even two at this stage of the bout was absolutely nothing; it was part of the natural ebb and flow of any contest. I had been attacking from too far away throughout the second round and I got caught with a couple of shots. Towards the end of the round, I started to get back into it and I landed with a one-two. But I needed to get closer when I was trying to score, if I attacked her from too far out, it was too easy for her to time her counter punches.

Round Three

We had prepared for this situation well in advance of the final, back in the gym in Bray and in my training camps leading up to the Games. I went into the third round knowing that I could turn it around, largely because Dad had hand-picked my sparring for this type of fight against a boxer like Ochigava. Before I came to London, I had been doing a lot of rounds with Eric Donavan, who is a brilliant Irish southpaw, and an established international boxer. He also came to the Olympic training camp in Assisi with me so I could get as much practice as possible against his southpaw, counter-attacking style.

Eric told me that he thought I was in the best shape of my life when we left Assisi. Dad has always tried to find the right sparring partners to help prepare for specific opponents, and we had done quite a lot of work with southpaws in the weeks before heading to London. Michael Nevin, another strong southpaw, was also brought in. He met John Joe Nevin (who went on to win a silver medal in

> **That ability to raise my level of performance had rarely been more crucial, and I did exactly that in the defining third round.**

the Olympics) in the finals of the Irish Senior Championships earlier in 2012.

I also sparred with Dean Walsh, who is the nephew of Ireland head coach Billy Walsh. He is a really tall boxer, and I had done some work with him in case I came up against the Chinese fighter Cheng Dong at some point during the Olympics. Cheng, at six feet, is one of the tallest fighters in the women's game.

Although it's never possible to completely imitate a fighter in training, I did try as much as possible to spar against people who adopted the same style as my likely opponents, or even found people with a similar body shape to work with. These small things can make a difference. And that is especially true when you consider that the guys I was training with were faster and stronger than anyone I was ever going to meet in the Olympic Games.

Lads like Eric Donovan and Bray club-mate Stephen Coughlan were exactly the calibre of spar I needed, and Dad would even remind me of the quality of my sparring partners to give me confidence before fights. When preparing me for Ochigava, he would say to me: 'This girl is nothing compared to Eric Donovan' or 'This girl isn't nearly as strong as the men you spar in the club.'

For years now, I have worked with some great-quality sparring partners in Ireland, boxers who were better than the girls I was competing against in championships. When you consider that among those I spar with are double Olympic bronze medallist Paddy Barnes, Olympic bronze flyweight Michael Conlan and even sometimes bantamweight silver medallist John Joe Nevin, you can see that I was working with the best that Ireland has to offer. There is no doubt that being surrounded by this kind of talent has played a part in my own success.

Sparring with the top male boxers doesn't make for an easy life when it comes to training, because I have to be able to raise my level

On the attack against Ochigava. In the third round I took a crucial lead in the bout.

to hold my own. But that's what you need in any sport: to push yourself hard when you practice. It's especially true in boxing, for as Dad says: 'In football if you have a bad day, you may lose a game, but in boxing if you have a bad day, somebody is probably punching you in the face!'

That ability to raise my level of performance had rarely been more crucial than it was now, and I did exactly that in the defining third round against Ochigava. By the end of the two minutes, I had overturned the deficit. I was now two points ahead overall after my best phase in the fight, with the score reading 7-5. I had to be more aggressive in the third round, but not in the same way I was against Jonas in the quarter-finals; this fight required a more controlled and tactical aggression. I was getting closer before letting off my combinations and then avoiding her attacks at the same time. I won the round 4-1. It was the pivotal spell in the contest and entirely changed the fight around in my favour. I knew then that she was going to have to move out of her normal pattern and attack me more in the last round if she wanted to win. I would have to be ready for her.

Round Four

The scales had tipped. She now had to chase me and everyone in the stadium knew she would be coming. It would make for a tense two minutes. I couldn't give away any cheap shots – one good shot could change the momentum and I couldn't let that happen during the final round. The last thing I wanted to give her now was a glimmer of hope.

I kept her on her toes all of the time during that last round with a series of feints. The two-point advantage was no more than a small cushion, but it had been clear throughout the whole week that the final round was generally win-or-bust for the chasing boxer as they tried to claw back the score. I knew that a bad spell of ten seconds could have changed the whole course of the fight, so it was probably the most cautious round of my life. I was reluctant even to exchange punches in case the judges saw her punches and not mine. I tried to stay out of reach, pumping out my left any time she stepped into range.

At the end of the fourth round, the bell sounded and I looked across at Dad and Zauri in the corner and asked 'Is it me?' I didn't know what the score was, but I was sure that it was close. It's not always easy to guess what way the judges are seeing a fight. Important incidents in the round raced through my mind: the couple of times we exchanged combinations, what way did the judges score them? What about when I slipped on the canvas, did they score that? Did I do enough to hold her off for the win?

I hadn't a clue how they would call it. I find it hard to judge fights when I'm actually in them. But at the end, Dad and Zauri were confident. They knew I was two points up going into the last two minutes and they thought the last round was pretty even, so they were confident it would be fine.

Usually the judges' decision is announced quickly once the fight is over. But this wasn't one of those days – it seemed to be taking ages for them to make their announcement. The delay didn't help my nerves. Dad kept reassuring me that the decision was going my way and that there was no way I lost the last round by two points, but the longer it went on, the more doubts ballooned in my head.

Then I thought the decision was going to a count-back, which is what happens when the judges score the fight even by the usual scoring method. We were waiting so long that Dad had stopped reassuring me and I think even he began to wonder if it was going to go to a count-back, and then the decision could be something of a lottery.

You could hear a pin drop in the stadium as we waited. The crowd had fallen from megaphone levels of uproar to a complete silence. Nobody knew what was happening. Finally, they began to announce the decision: 'And the winner of that contest by a score . . .' I'm waiting to hear the words 'in the red corner', but before I could

As the referee raises my arm, I sink to my knees in joy.

make out what was said, the crowd had erupted in pandemonium at the announcement. Then I felt the referee begin to raise my right arm, and I knew it was me . . . I was the Olympic champion!

Olympic Champion

In moments like that, the regular emotions seem almost redundant. My feelings were supernatural. I dropped to my knees in tears with my arms lifted high over my head. I took a moment to close my eyes and thank my God. Opening my eyes, I tried to take in the accomplishment of a lifetime's ambition and to absorb the noise and the lights and the atmosphere of the ExCeL Arena.

There was more than sheer joy, there was a sense of deep satisfaction, too. I had done the hard work for years in the gym and endured months of expectation coming up to London. I had put pressure on myself and my family to get here, and I had campaigned to get women's boxing into the Olympics. I had been dreaming about winning gold at the Olympics for years. Even before the Olympic qualifiers in China, people were talking to me about winning medals at the Olympic Games. It got to the point where I was almost feeling that my Olympic dream had become the nation's dream and failure to win would crush everyone's hopes, not just my own. While I tried to remain self-contained and to remove myself from other people's demands, I still felt an overwhelming need to please the crowd.

Dad reaches out to congratulate me: a dream fulfilled as it sinks in that I am an Olympic champion.

Then, as all the emotions flooded into my head, I jumped around the ring in delight, something I never do. To see my dad in my corner, with the emotion welling up in his eyes, bursting with joy and pride was amazing. When I picked myself up from the canvas, I went straight over to him, he kissed my head and I gave him a big hug. Neither of us is particularly expressive, so to see him and Zauri jumping around like children when the decision was announced is imprinted in my mind forever.

I stood on the side of the ring and stared up into the stands, where hundreds of flashes and camera phones twinkled back at me.

Sharing the moment of victory with the wonderful fans who had supported me.

As I left the arena, I walked through the crowd and people shouted at me and held out their hands. Many of them had left their seats and pushed down to the front where I was walking out and they waved their scarves at me. I looked up into the crowd and could see the green tracksuits of the Irish lads, who were up where they usually sat, along with Sonia O'Sullivan and others from the Irish team.

As I was about to leave the arena via the media tunnel, I could see a row of cameras pointing at me and a lot of happy faces staring out at me. I think I posed a few times for photographs and shook some hands. I wasn't really thinking about what I was doing; I was just trying to soak up everything – smiling, grinning and pinching myself to make sure it was all real. I wasn't ready to leave the arena just yet; I wanted to stay there forever with the thousands of people who had travelled over to support me.

Finally, I had to go. I had a schedule of interviews and the mandatory trip to doping, which usually takes me ages after a fight. All of that took maybe an hour, before I came out for the medal ceremony and for the national anthem. Again I experienced the same reaction from the crowds.

Although I had been able to sit back and take it in for a while behind the scenes, I was still in a daze. For the medal ceremony, I just followed the person in front of me towards the podium. Coincidentally, she was actually from Donegal and she came out grinning from ear to ear. The crowd were in party mode.

Adriana, Mavzuna, myself and Sofya at the medal ceremony.

That day, everything seemed to be about the Irish, because they outnumbered everybody else in the arena. There was another eruption of noise when Pat Hickey put the gold medal around my neck. I finally had it, my gold medal, and it was beautiful. I'll never forget that feeling of pride and accomplishment. I thought about all of those things that go into making a moment like that: my country, my faith, my sport, my ambition – and Mam and Dad always there in my corner. It was also about the Olympics and what they meant to me and fulfilling that dream I had as a child. When I recall the medal presentation, even months later, I still get emotional.

I don't think there was a dry eye in the place. I never heard the national anthem, *Amhrán na bhFiann*, sung so loudly. It was an emotional moment for my family as they all stood proudly, arm in arm, in the ExCeL Arena. A friend of Mam's said that her mother stood up for the anthem in her sitting room back in Ireland. When the medal ceremony was over, the medallists were led back to the media area, and someone threw an Irish flag down to me. I wrapped myself in the Irish tri-colour and began to do a lap around the arena as thousands sang out 'Ole, Ole, Ole!' The moment felt iconic, it felt bigger than me.

Meanwhile, thousands more had been watching my bout back home on giant screens set up by the Shoreline Leisure Centre in Bray.

Huge crowds turned out to watch my final on a big screen back in Bray.

The organisers even had shuttle buses taking people from the train station so they could be there. I even heard that the telephone exchange in Kilcoole, a small town a few miles

That evening of 9 August 2012, the past and present finally caught up with me.

along the coast from where I live, fell quiet during the fight, only to resume normal service when it had finished. Wherever people were, they were getting caught up in the atmosphere.

It had been a long road, and there were some tough times along the way, but the years I have been competing have been a privilege for me. As I've gone on, I have learned a great deal about myself and I have grown as a boxer and as a person because of those experiences. But I'm not done yet – there is plenty more still to come from me.

If my Olympic journey was a life-enhancing trip to every corner of my emotions, I am honoured and touched that it seems to have been important to people in Ireland, and especially the people of Bray, as well. As I was closeted in London for more than two weeks, I still can't fully appreciate what went on around Dublin city or on the Bray seafront or back home in my estate in Oldcourt.

I have seen clips of the crowds that gathered to watch my fights on big screens, I have been shown some images taken on smart phones from the final against Ochigava, and I've looked at recordings of the fans celebrating after the fight in the ExCeL Arena. In all of them, what strikes me is the buoyancy of the mood and joy of everyone. As people have shared their memories of those moments with me, or I've watched back some of the footage, I've occasionally wished that I had been there, that I could also have been part of that Olympic Games party and that . . . Then suddenly I remember: hold on a second, I was the one that won the gold medal! I *was* there, but it just didn't seem like I was.

That evening of 9 August 2012, the past and present finally caught up with me. I hadn't slept well all week, but now that I had

How proud I was to be wearing that gold medal.

won the night was just beginning. Straight after the formalities in the ExCeL, things tumbled forward at pace and I was whisked all over the place. After the medal ceremony, I went into London for various television requests, including an interview with Irish broadcaster RTE.

Celebrating in my Own Way

Once those duties were completed, we travelled to The Irish House in the centre of London, where there was a party in full swing going on near King's Cross train station. When I arrived, the crowd just surged forward and people were jumping up on the stage to get a better view. I was tired, and things were crazy and hectic, but I was glad to be there because it was an opportunity to show my face for a short while, and make a small gesture of thanks to some of the Irish supporters who had given me such unbelievable backing.

Eventually we slipped away and I felt the night beginning to come to a close. But as it did, hunger knocked. We'd made no grand plans, and before I knew it we were outside a McDonald's near Trafalgar Square in the centre of London. It was almost closing time, but we went in and sat by the window where there were a few free stools. Just the four of us were there, Mam and Dad, my sister Sarah and me, and we ate a chicken nugget meal. As if it had been just a normal day, we sat there looking out of the window at the throngs of people going by, hurrying to catch the night buses home or trying to hail a taxi. But I was sat inside with my family, my Olympic gold medal shoved deep into my tracksuit pocket, and for me, it was a perfect end to a perfect day.

The day after the final, every Irish newspaper had a picture of me on the front page, while on the front of almost every English paper

British boxer Nicola Adams was smiling out at the readers. Just imagine: women's boxing was headlining the newspapers in two countries! A sport that hadn't been allowed in the Olympics before now was suddenly getting so much attention. It said something about the impact that its inclusion in the Olympics had on the general public. Suddenly Nicola Adams and I were getting a massive amount of coverage, and it was brilliant for the sport we both love.

> Acceptance into the Olympics has broken down many of the barriers in the sport, but we still have a way to go.

There is still work to be done, however. Acceptance into the Olympics has broken down many of the barriers in the sport, but we still have a way to go before changing people's perceptions of women in boxing.

As recently as the 2010 World Championships in Barbados, we were still trying to fight archaic prejudices in our sport. After a technical meeting prior to the competition beginning in Barbados, the officials informed us that we had to wear skirts in the ring during our fights and then proceeded to hand them out to the girls. I can't remember what stupid reasons they were offering for this demeaning insult, but I refused to do so and said I would not defend my title if they insisted on it.

By the Olympic Games, we had come along way, and I think we stepped through those ropes not as girls trying their hand at a man's game, but as equals. We were simply boxers.

Now, my Olympic journey was over, and I could finally relax, though I still couldn't sleep. By eight o'clock the next morning, I was texting Dad to see how he was. Even though it had been a late night, he was already up, but he was surprised to hear from me, as he thought I'd be enjoying a well-earned sleep.

'Do you want to go for a walk?' I asked.

CHAPTER 7

THE GOOD NEWS

I'm just passing on the good news!

Finding Faith

My faith. I have always talked openly about my Christian faith. Nowadays, it seems that talking about Jesus has become a private or personal matter, it's almost taboo to talk about Him in public. But for me, it is natural to talk about God, because my faith is not separate from every other aspect of my life; instead it is central to every aspect, and that includes boxing. I know people have questioned why I'm always thanking God after every fight, but it's natural to acknowledge the people who have helped you achieve something great, and I know more than I know anything else that I wouldn't have an Olympic gold medal if I did not have God in my life.

I have also heard people say that boxing isn't a sport that a Christian should become involved in because of the aggressive and physical nature of the sport. My view is that people who say those things know neither boxing nor the heart of God, because I believe that it is God who has given me this talent for boxing. I believe this is a gift and that it is my God-given destiny to be a boxer. For me that is absolutely clear. I'm privileged to glorify His name through my boxing. To say that Christianity and boxing are incompatible also misses the point that the aim in boxing is to outscore an opponent, not to hurt them.

Besides, God isn't exactly squeamish when it comes to fighting and there are plenty of references to combat in the scriptures.

(*Previous page*)
Medal ceremony.

Some of the great men of the Bible, such as David, Gideon and Samson, are men of war. Look at how Jesus drove the money-changers out of the temple. He is ferocious. Of all of the characters in the Bible, I particularly enjoy reading about David, because he was such a warrior and a man of great courage and integrity. He is the only person in the Bible described as a man after God's own heart, which says a lot about who David was, but also a lot about who God is. Most of the psalms are written by David, I find them all incredibly powerful and I often recite them when I'm preparing for a fight.

'He trains my hands for battle; my arms can bend a bow of bronze. You make your saving help my shield . . .'

When you read the scriptures closely, you begin to realise that Jesus is far removed from people's soft-focus perception of a serene, bearded man in flimsy sandals, some sort of Jewish Gandhi figure. In fact, Jesus is a mighty warrior, He's not called the Lion of Judah for nothing!

God's promises through the scriptures are relevant to me in how I approach my boxing, but they are also central to my life and who I am. Over the last few years certain scriptures have really spoken to me and given me an assurance that God has a great plan for me. The one that really stands out is my favourite Psalm 18, which I love so much that it has become known among my friends and family as 'Katie's Psalm', it says. 'It is God who arms me with strength and keeps my way secure. He makes my feet like the feet of a deer; He causes me to stand on the heights. He trains my hands for battle; my arms can bend a bow of bronze. You make your saving help my shield . . .'

There are others that seemed to have relevance for my sport: 'My heart and flesh may fail, but God is the strength of my heart and my portion forever.' and 'The Lord is my strength and my shield,

> Some might suggest that I have an agenda when I talk about God, but when I'm thanking God in public, I am simply honouring God for what He's done.

my heart trusts in Him.' These are the words that have really inspired and encouraged me over the years. Every time I have to box, I speak these truths over and over throughout the entire day. They gave me the strength and the confidence to get through the hours and minutes leading up to the Olympic final. I wouldn't be able to deal with the pressures and expectations without Him by my side.

While some people are uncomfortable with the topic of religion and faith, this is not true of everyone. Over the last few months, I have received hundreds of letters and cards relating to my faith from complete by strangers. Of course I got the odd card saying that it is not God who helped me to win gold at the World Championships or Olympic Games, but the vast majority are overwhelmingly supportive of me and my openness about my faith.

I know it was just a throw-away comment by the Irish American comedian Des Bishop but he tweeted: 'Katie Taylor would turn an atheist back to God.' I think it's a good thing for people to feel comfortable about talking about God in public – after all, we talk openly about everything else.

I do recognise that we have a complex relationship with religion in Ireland, that there is a history of conflict in the name of religion and denominationalism and that this has had an impact on how we think about faith, but the amount of positive responses about me being open about my faith has been encouraging. Some might suggest that I have an agenda when I talk about God, but when I'm thanking God in public, I am simply honouring God for what He's done. If people don't agree with me then that's OK.

The Family Story

For as long as I can remember, I've always had a measure of faith. My mam first became a Christian before I was born, so we were used to church and Bible stories growing up, but at some point you have to make your own decisions about what you believe, and I have done that.

Mam's faith began when she was 12 or 13 years old. She was brought up in Wolftone, an area about five minutes from where we live in Bray, and was raised in what people might now call a dysfunctional family. There wasn't a lot of money in the family and her father, my grandfather, had a drink problem, which is not an unusual story in Ireland.

One day, a Christian couple named Robin and Olive Boles, were knocking on doors of the houses in the area, inviting the kids to a youth club they were starting up. Mam and a gang of her friends ended up straggling along out of curiosity. It was in that youth club that she first heard that God wasn't a distant and angry figure, but that He was a loving father who wanted a relationship with His children. That was a completely different God to the one she was taught about in school, where God was portrayed as watching her every move, waiting for a mistake so He could punish her. She says she didn't feel good enough to be loved by that God. But with Robin and Olive, she knew she was loved and accepted, and the God they spoke about was a God that wasn't out to lash her every time she put a foot wrong.

The Boles really left their mark on Mam, and I might not have come to know God today if not for their kindness. Mam was still a teenager when she first met my dad, and at this stage she had drifted from the youth club. They had known each other for only six months when they got married. They were both pretty crazy when they were younger, so life was sometimes turbulent. By the time Mam was 24 years old, they had four children. She was two years younger than I am now and she had four kids, I can't imagine that!

> You have to make your own decisions about what you believe, and I have done that.

With the pressures of life and looking after four young children, she drifted away from God, church and the Boles family. Her return came only after a tragic incident that jarred her soul more than anything else in her life up until then. One St Stephen's Day night in the mid-1990s, a fire broke out in one of the nearby houses on our road in Oldcourt. My older brother Lee woke up first and ran in to my parents' room, saying there was a fire just outside. They got up and looked out. Flames were bursting out of the Cassidys' home just a few doors down from us. Everyone was on the street. Dad went around the back of the burning house with some other men to see if they could get in. They didn't know if anybody was still in there.

The fire brigade arrived and got to work, and it soon became apparent that there were still people trapped inside. The mother along with four of the five children were killed. I was too young at the time to understand the scale of the tragedy, I just knew that something awful had happened. It had a terrible effect on my mam and I think she really struggled to get her head around it. It became a turning point in her thinking.

Number Five

Walking through Bray the next day, she decided to go for a cup of coffee in a little basement café on Eglinton Road called Crack Pots. It turned out that the coffee shop was being run as a charity for a small church upstairs. And who was running the charity but Olive Boles.

With my sister-in-law Kim and my niece Madeleine Hope Taylor.

Peter getting his PhD at University College Dublin.

With my nephew Jake.

With my nephews Jason, Leon, Aaron and Jake.

With my mam, dad and brother Lee after winning the WWBC in 2010.

My nephews Aaron and Jason.

With my cousin Lauren.

Me and my friend Susan Byrne.

My nanny and aunt Aileen with the Olympic torch!

With my nephew Aaron.

My niece Madeleine.

My sister Sarah and my sister-in-law Nicola.

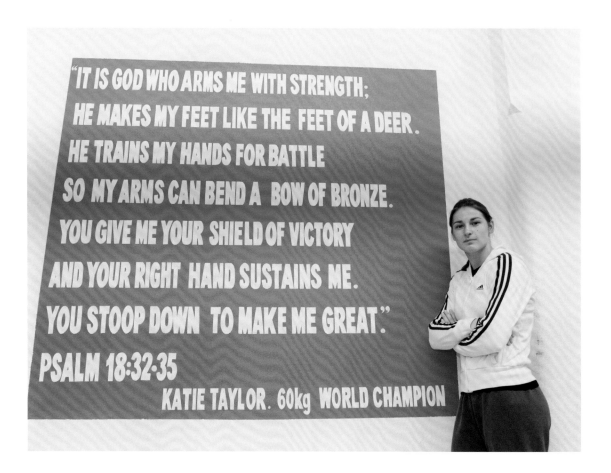

Extracts from my favourite psalm on the wall of the national boxing stadium in Dublin.

Some appointments are divine! After running into Olive, Mam began attending the church there, which Robin and Olive were actively involved in running. We affectionately called the church 'Number Five' since that was the building's address.

Going to Number Five was my first introduction to church, and I have a lot of great memories from the years we attended there. The church provided a wonderful sense of community and belonging. We felt we were part of the fabric of the place, it wasn't just a place we came to once a week, sang a few songs, said a few prayers and left. We were family. I think things started to change for our own family from that point, things seemed less crazy at home. There was a stability that wasn't there before.

Creating that stable environment for us became really important for Mam and Dad. At that time, during the 1990s, Oldcourt was struggling with drug-related problems and some good people lost loved ones to tragedies involving heroin overdoses or suicide. I think my parents understood that sport was a way out of that kind of life and that it could provide a focus for their kids. So they were always encouraging us to get involved in sports of all kinds. As a child, I was oblivious to whatever problems or social issues were going on in my estate; I loved growing up there, it's my home and my neighbours have supported me from the first time I put on Dad's old gloves to spar with the boys on the bank outside our house.

> As a child, I was oblivious to whatever problems or social issues were going on in my estate; I loved growing up there.

Mam never took the stance that the point of Christianity is attending church. So when I started playing football and there was a clash between my games and church services, she was willing to let me miss church. Then during the off-season, or when my game was cancelled, I'd go to church at Number Five.

I had such an appetite for competition even then, and I loved the discipline aspect of sport. I enjoyed training hard.Iit sounds weird that a little girl of eight or nine years old should enjoy a tough session but I did, and I took my sport seriously. When a life of discipline has a focus and a purpose, it is much easier to live it out, and I always felt like the disciplined life I was living was making me a better athlete.

At around the time when my friends started drinking, when most people start to feel peer pressure, it really didn't seem to have any pull on me. I loved the way I was living. I was living an exciting life. And in fairness to my friends, they respected what I thought and they never pressurised me to drink. Anyway I was too busy. I don't think there was a single evening in a normal week where I didn't have a match or training session to be at.

St Mark's

We had been going to Number Five for a number of years, probably the best part of a decade. Then Olive became very sick; they discovered a brain tumour. She, along with her husband Robin, were the backbone of the church and I think it was probably hard for Robin to look after the church and Olive at the same time. Eventually though, Olive died and the church kind of slowly disbanded. Mam was very close to Olive, and I think it's probably the most broken-hearted I've ever seen her.

It was just before Number Five dissolved that Mam started going into St Mark's Church on Pearse Street in Dublin's city centre on Sunday evenings. It would be a few years before we called St Mark's home. A group from Number Five had started to attend a local church in Bray called Mountainview that met in St Andrew's School. We went there on and off for a while. At the time, I was happy enough just playing football on a Sunday and tagging along with Mam whenever I didn't have a game. Eventually, though, my curiosity and hunger started to grow; I was also becoming more aware that I needed God. I always knew that on some level, but it was really starting to sink in.

My family with our church pastor Sean Mullarkey.

Mam also wanted us to put our roots down somewhere and she felt as though St Mark's was the right place. It was there that my faith and my relationship with God really started to grow.

Mark's, as we call it, was different to any church we'd been to before. It's an inner-city church. There's history in the area and in the building. The congregation are such a mixed bunch, with people from every nationality and every walk of life. In Mark's you have passers-by coming in off the streets. There is a real feeling of outreach and they're constantly trying to do things to serve the local community. That's what church should be: loving and serving people, not just those that agree with your view, loving everybody.

Our church has gone through such a difficult time over the past couple of years, with sickness and tragedies affecting some of those who come in regularly. But still you see the families of those that have died praising God week in week out, even though their hearts are broken. That's the sort of Christian I want to be. They have gone through such a difficult time and they don't understand why, and yet they still come in and give thanks to God. That's just inspiring for me. I learn from those people.

Mark's is now one of my favourite places to be. I love going in there on Sundays. The presence of God in the place is amazing and I love the worship there. My sister-in-law Kim, my brother Peter's wife, is the director of the music and worship in the church. She, like my mam, is a great woman of God. She's given me so many words of encouragement over the last few years that have really helped me through some major championships. Everyone in Mark's has been so supportive, I'm convinced I wouldn't be where I am today without their prayers.

St Mark's is what church should be: loving and serving people, not just those that agree with your view, loving everybody.

'The Lord is my Strength and my Shield' on my boxing robe.

My pastor, Sean Mullarkey, and the assistant pastor, Anna Tormey, always pray with me before I go away to a tournament. On the Sunday before I went to London for the Games, Anna's husband was terminally ill and had only a few days left to live, and Anna still came over and prayed with me. That's church! People fighting for your dreams like that, even in the midst of their own struggles, I'll never forget Anna's sacrifice for me that morning. The whole church was praying for me when I was in London, it was so encouraging, I needed it.

Village Prayer

I'm a creature of habit and I usually feel out of sorts if I don't get to go to church for a few weeks, so I was delighted when a letter was dropped into my room from one of the pastors in the Olympic Village to say there were a few services going on during the Games. He had heard that I was a Christian.

There was an area in the village called the Faith Centre. They had a room for Buddhists if they wanted to meet, another room for Hindus and one for Christians, different rooms for different religions. The first time I went was midweek. There were only a handful of people there. One of the Jamaican sprinters was there, Sam Henry-Robinson was her name. She went on to win a silver medal with the 4x100 relay team.

I really enjoyed the service so I went back on the Sunday morning, and this time the place was jammed with athletes. The service was run by the athletes themselves, many of them got up and shared a story of something amazing God had done for them. Brigetta Barrett from the USA was there, she won a silver medal in the high jump. Another girl from New Zealand stood up and told how she was the first from her country to ever qualify in her swimming event, and she thanked God for that. The 400m runner LaShawn Merritt, who had won gold at the Beijing Olympics, was there too. The common denominator was God working for them. There was something powerful about that. I found it to be emotional just listening to people speaking about how God helped them. Apart from winning the gold medal, this was probably my stand-out experience of the Games.

> Although I do try my best, I sometimes do find it hard to express myself. I am a quiet person by nature.

I'm not really one for talking. I'm a woman of a few words. For me, the interviews are harder than the fights! People are always asking me to do talks within different churches. That's just not who I am, this side of things doesn't come naturally. I believe actions speak louder than words. I was told that Irish rugby captain Brian O'Driscoll says that as well. Although I do try my best, I sometimes do find it hard to express myself. I am a quiet person by nature. I never feel comfortable standing up on a podium and being asked to address a crowd, trying to put all my feelings and emotions into words. When people talk to you they sometimes expect you to know all the answers. But I don't.

What I do know is that with any of the struggles that I've gone through, I have always looked to the scriptures and I've always found something. I don't understand absolutely everything that's written in the Bible and so I know that people can have doubts and reservations. There is that famous Mark Twain line that goes 'It's not the things I don't understand in the scriptures that worry me, it's the things that I do understand.'

The scriptures aren't to be read like a philosophy book. They are there to point you to the person of Christ. It's that relationship that's the point. If I was pushed into summing them up in one sentence, I would say that the scriptures are a love letter from God to man. It's about the grace of God and His mercy. I feel I have a new start every day with God. It's not about being judgemental, I don't for a second think that I'm better or 'holier' than anybody else. We are an ordinary family and we make mistakes every single day. I'm simply saying that I know someone who can help you change your life beyond your wildest dreams, and His name is Jesus.

They are the things I believe in. I know people are always going to hold strong opinions on issues of faith, whatever their religion, because that's human nature. I understand that faith can be a contentious issue and also that everyone is entitled to an opinion. But ultimately you can't argue with someone's personal relationship with a God who is real to them, a relationship is undeniable. For us, it started with somebody simply telling us that a relationship with God is possible. I'm just passing on the good news!

Meeting the stars of the future at St John's boxing club in Cork.

CHAPTER 8

THE
HOMECOMING

Knocked out by the Irish.

Bus Ride through Bray

Of all the places I have been around the world, there is nowhere more beautiful than Ireland on a blue-sky, summer's day. When the plane back from London landed in Dublin airport and I took my first step out onto the top of the steps, it felt good to be home.

Almost as soon as the Olympic final was over, I found that I was eager to make the journey home. I couldn't even wait for the plane to land to breathe the famous Irish air. I had peered out of the opened cockpit window of the jet, as it was parked in the bay, posing for photographs with my gold medal, and I could see the commotion on the apron outside. Then, the doors of the plane were opened and the five of us who had won medals, including bronze medal-winning showjumper Cian O'Connor, were ushered forward to step out into the Dublin air with our gold, silver and bronze medals around our necks and a posse of photographers looking on. Little did I know that this was the beginning of a long day, but I wouldn't have chosen to be anywhere else in the world.

My schedule for the next few hours had been broadly laid out and took in the official welcome home at the airport, a press conference and, after that, a journey back to Bray. I was rolling with everything and, since the medal ceremony, it seemed I was blindly running from one event to the other. In Bray, I was told there would be some people

waiting to welcome Adam Nolan and me home. I'd no idea then of the scale of the welcome that was waiting for us, or that I was about to experience one of the most emotional days of my life – it seemed as though the last week had been full of them.

Mam had been sent some texts from Bray to let her know that there would be 'something' happening on the seafront. Dad was in touch with his friend John Murphy and Pat Devlin, an adviser, and he had asked them to run everything by him. So he was well informed about what the plan was, but even he couldn't have imagined the scale of the celebration. Officially, Bray Council was running the event and had organised an open-top bus ride through the town and down to the seafront where there was live music playing on the bandstand.

My mind turned to Bray as soon as we landed in Dublin airport, but there were still some formalities, such as a press conference to

With my fellow medal winners Michael Conlan, John Joe Nevin and Paddy Barnes at Dublin airport.

The whole way through the town, they cheered and clapped. I was overwhelmed by it all.

do, before I was whisked out to St Brendan's School, which is just outside the town near Woodbrook Golf Club, to board the open-top bus. Some of my family were waiting for us there. As the bus moved off and we reached the edge of town, we began to see groups of people lining the streets, thinly at first, but as we went deeper into the centre of Bray the numbers started to swell. Very quickly the crowd snowballed in size, lining the streets five or six rows deep. The whole way through the town, they cheered and clapped. I had my gold medal around my neck and all I could do was smile and wave. I was overwhelmed by it all.

As we turned down the Quinsborough Road towards the sea, both sides of the street were filled with people; the sun was shining and the mood was electric. It was an incredible scene, with balloons and flags and tee-shirts with my face printed on them. Kids were screaming and trying to run along the crowded footpath to keep up with the bus. Every now and then, I'd spot a friend in the crowds and I'd point to my medal as if to say: 'Can you believe I did it!'

If we thought it was packed on the Quinsborough Road, it was nothing compared to when the bus reached the beach, crossing the train tracks by the station. Over to the left, towards the harbour, was Bray Boxing Club, our little gym that minted this gold medal, and straight ahead was the path by the sea where Adam, the lads and I had jogged together so many times over the years.

Everything here was familiar to me: the buildings, the sea, the whole terrain, but my mind was struggling to soak it all in as the bus slowly turned onto the wide-open seafront. This was our first glimpse of the masses that had gathered around the iconic bandstand that hosts the music acts during the summer festival. I looked up towards the Martello Tower at the far end of Bray and all I could see were thousands upon thousands of bobbing heads. I was exhausted after two hard weeks in London and several tough months of preparation, but right then it didn't matter: these people had come to see me, and had supported me throughout my career, long before I became an Olympian.

As I tried to take in the sight, all I could think about was how on earth I was going to get off the bus and onto the bandstand, where Adam and I would address the crowd. Fortunately the organisers, who were brilliant on the day, had put safety barriers in place to usher us onto the bandstand without being mobbed by the supporters. We were told there were 20,000 there to greet us, which is amazing since Bray is home to about 30,000. People were everywhere: in the gardens, hanging out from their windows, in the pubs and restaurants, and lining every piece of the footpath up to the top end.

It was such a party atmosphere as we drove through the streets of Bray.

As I toured through Bray with Dad, everyone wanted to catch a glimpse of my gold medal.

I saw many more in their Katie tee-shirts. On a patch of grass, I saw two kids dressed in the Irish football kit hitting each other with giant green boxing gloves with 'Knocked out by the Irish' printed in black letters. I could have been looking at myself 18 years ago on the bank. I was delighted to see so many kids there, as I hoped that what I had done might inspire them to dream big dreams.

The bus continued slowly along the road towards the Martello, with a squad car and two police outriders on motorcycles leading the way. Policemen walked alongside the bus between the barriers helping to ensure we could squeeze through the crowds. When we arrived at the Martello, we saw a giant banner of Adam and me hanging on the outside wall. In the background, the sun was shining on Bray Head. I always miss the mountains when I'm away. It was a day you would have wanted to be outside, and it seemed that almost everybody in Bray was.

The beachfront is a beautiful place, especially in the summer when it is buzzing with lots of people. There is a pebbly beach where many go swimming and a broad walkway that runs the length of the promenade. At one end, at the foot of Bray Head where the amusement arcades are located, there is a walk that winds around the cliffs by the sea for a few miles to the neighbouring seaside town of Greystones. All I could see along the front were people cheering and shouting at me, and the clear outline of the cliffs and pastures of Bray Head behind. Just then, a plane flew across the bay with a banner trailing out the back reading: 'Congratulations.' I was beginning to feel emotional again.

The crowds at the seafront in Bray turned up in their thousands to welcome us home – it was a special moment.

The Bandstand and the Martello

The stage was set up at the old bandstand, an iconic landmark around Bray. RTE's Des Cahill was waiting to greet us, along with a group called The Camembert Quartet, famous for being the in-house band on *The Late Late Show*. I'd met them before when I've been on the chat show. They played lots of well-known rock ballads and retro eighties tunes that they had rewritten to include my name somewhere in the chorus.

As I've said, the organisers did a great job, striking a balance between allowing the crowds a certain amount of access to what was happening, while at the same time giving us enough room to be able to enjoy it and to engage with family and close friends. It was great to be able to address the crowds too, and to thank them for their unbelievable support, which I did during the interviews with Des on the bandstand. But not for the first time over these few days, the emotions were overwhelming and I was choking on my words. I'm not usually an emotional person, but then there was nothing usual about what we were seeing.

The scale of it wasn't like anything I had ever experienced, and although just about everyone wanted to have some kind of access to us on the day, I didn't mind at all. I wanted them to feel part of it – after all, the people of Bray *were* part of it. I was dazed and staggered that a women's boxing medal could generate such interest. It was more like Jack Charlton's football team arriving back from the USA World Cup.

On the bandstand, I was trying my best to put into words what this support meant to me, but as everyone knows words are not my strong point. But I think my tears spoke volumes. I told the crowd that the medal belonged to everyone and that without their support I wouldn't be in the position I was, that I wouldn't have won the gold medal without all the backing I had received over the past couple of weeks. I thanked all those from Bray who had travelled to London to shout me on in the ExCeL Arena and who played their part

The scale of it wasn't like anything I had ever experienced, and although just about everyone wanted to have some kind of access to us on the day, I didn't mind at all.

in registering the highest decibel reading at the Games, a fact that still blows my mind. I ended by saying that I felt like a whole nation had been praying for me and that I had felt the power and presence of God in that stadium. A shower of confetti and streamers then burst over my head.

From the bandstand we went into the Martello pub, where they had organised a semi-private function. Dad had made it clear we didn't want it to be a political affair there or on the bus, and we didn't want anyone to make a political speech. No agendas, just a celebration. It was a homecoming and we wanted to keep it that way as much as possible. We did go to a local restaurant, The Barracuda, for coffee, and while we were there we had photographs taken with some of the local politicians, but that was all. We didn't stay there for long and left to be escorted by six security guards back through the crowd to the Martello.

We were able to make that short journey without incident, although I think Mam got a bit panicked at one point, seeing so many trying to get a piece of her baby daughter, which is what I'll always be to her. There were some parents almost throwing their children in front of me for photographs, and she was worried about whether they were going to get too excited and start rushing at us. I think she was waiting for some sort of disaster to happen, or that someone might get crushed.

Choking back the tears as the confetti flutters in the breeze at Bray bandstand.

In contrast to the frenzy outside, it was relatively calm when we got back to the function room in the Martello. There were about a hundred people in there, mostly family and friends I'd grown up with, but also a few dignitaries and other invited guests. They had very generously put on some food for us, and there was an open bar all night – the bottles of champagne were flowing, not that I was drinking any, but it created a sense of occasion. It was important to me that those I had trained with all of my life were there too, so I was delighted that many of my club-mates from Bray Boxing Club were able to join us.

By about 9.20, it was getting dark and we were led from the function room up to the roof to watch the firework display over the beach. By now I must admit I was beginning to fade. It had been impossible for me to eat anything, as everyone seemed to want a picture of me and the medal, or me and Adam together, or else they wanted their kids photographed with the medal. I was happy to oblige. Lots of the kids were picking up my medal to feel its weight, and the reaction was always the same: 'Wow! That's heavy. Is it solid gold?' When I put it in the flat of my hand, it covered the entire area of my palm. It was a joy to be home showing off my gold medal.

Reflections on China

It was only now that I could stop and think. I had been going at it hard since long before the World Championships in China, way back to the start of the year. That was eight months before this party, and the cumulative effect of all that work and tension was probably catching up with me. People didn't perhaps understand how important China was and how intensely I had prepared for it. It was all very well fighting in the glare of the Olympic Games, with what seemed like the entire country standing behind me at every move, but my boxing life has more often been about me and Dad on our own in a strange country coping with a different culture. Usually these tournaments are long and lonely weeks, with no glamour, no television cameras and no screaming fans cheering to lift us.

I remember that when we arrived in China, I was conscious that this was going to be the most important tournament of my life. If things hadn't gone well for me, there would have been no Olympic Games and no gold medal. Public and media perceptions at that time irritated me, because all anyone spoke about before I went to Qinhuangdao was the Olympic Games, not the World Championships. But the event in China was also doubling as the London 2012 qualifier, so if it didn't happen for me there in China, there would be no London Games for me.

So many people assumed that I would be going to box in the Olympics come what may, but that wasn't the case. I had to qualify in China first. For those early months of the year, I didn't want to talk about the ExCeL or Stratford or the Olympic Park, and I didn't want to assume going to London 2012 was a formality. It wasn't a given – I had to earn my place like anyone else. But my name had been associated with Ireland's Olympic campaign long before I qualified. I was even our favourite for a medal before I qualified, and I'd be lying if I said I didn't feel the pressure of this level of expectation.

Far away from the Irish crowds, China provided its own emotional swings and was different from any tournament I'd ever been involved in. The competition had a uniquely stressful element to it, because qualification for London depended not just on how I did but also on how everybody else in the draw finished up. I could have qualified after one fight or two, depending on how girls from other countries were progressing.

> So many people assumed that I would be going to box in the Olympics come what may, but that wasn't the case. I had to qualify in China first.

The reason for that was that the International Olympic Committee had drawn up a quota system to make sure countries from all over the world were represented in the Olympic Games. They didn't want the final competition in the ExCeL to be stuffed with boxers from the strongest continents, such as Europe, and possibly no athlete from Africa or Australia. That made it different to anything I'd been in before, because I had to do things that aren't normally part of my competition routine: assessing how everyone else was performing and trying to work out how they fitted into the quota system. I don't usually care or bother myself with how the other girls in my weight are doing.

When we got to the last 16 of the World Championships, there were still ten European boxers left in the competition, which will give you some idea of the dominance of Europe in amateur boxing and what it takes to win a European title. Only four of them were knocked

Some people forget how important the World Championships were for me in 2012 – a poor tournament and I would have missed the Olympics.

out by the quarter-finals, and I began to wonder how many more fights I would have to win to go through to London. In the end, it was possible I might even have had to secure a place in the finals to be certain of qualifying for the Olympics, depending on the outcome of Mavzuna Chorieva's fight against the French girl Estelle Mosselly. But as luck would have it, Miheala Lacatus, my opponent from Romania, pulled out injured and I was given the bye to the semi-finals.

Dad watched the contest between Chorieva and Mosselly while I was pacing up and down in the dressing rooms; I couldn't watch. I generally don't look at the other fights, but I knew the result was crucial to what I needed to achieve. Then Dad ran down to me saying: 'Katie! You have qualified for the Olympic Games! You've qualified!'

Initially I didn't believe him, but Chorieva had won her fight 20-12 and, as she was from Tajikistan, the quota system favoured me and I was through. It was a strange feeling, because after years of battling for this chance to compete in the Olympics, I had got there without the drama of qualification resting on my result in the semi-finals. It was nice to catch a break and also it meant I could be completely focused now on retaining my world title, without having one eye on London.

It was an emotional moment; I would have my chance to fulfil my dream of an Olympic gold medal. Often in the past, tears had flowed thinking about whether my chance would ever come.

We were delighted and I allowed myself a moment to enjoy the status of an Olympian, but I knew my job in China wasn't complete, because it was important for me to travel to London as the current world champion. So it was back to business. Our first goal in China had been qualification for the Olympics, but our second goal was to win my fourth World Championship. If I hadn't gone on to beat Chorieva first in the semi-final (16-6) then Sofya Ochigava 11-7 in the final to become world champion again, it would have put a cloud over everything and I would have fought in London in a completely different frame of mind.

Most people find it easier to go into a big fight as the underdog, and it's true that there is less pressure to deal with, but I cherish being the favourite. For me, it gives me confidence that I am rated above my opponent, it is the privilege of being the best. I wouldn't have wanted to be standing facing Ochigava on final day in the ExCeL Arena as the second best boxer in the world, give me the pressure and expectation of being the best any day.

On the flight home to Dublin, Dad started his planning while I took ten days off to recover from the tournament. After that, I got my head down to work for London.

Back Home to Oldcourt

Peaking to win the World Championships and Olympics in the space of 12 weeks emptied me, but the energy of the fans and the overwhelming bus ride along the seafront among the people who I knew and who supported me was such a prized day in my life and a humbling one, too. The passage home was a celebration of where I came from and of what God had given me.

It was late when we finally left the seafront. We sneaked out the back and went to visit Nanny Kathleen, who lives nearby. She's now 80 years old, and I had not seen her for four weeks and she was the person I missed most while in London. She is a huge part of my life and if I win a medal in any championship, she is the first person I go round to see when I come home. I usually can't wait to show off my new medal to her. Her house is like the hub for the family and everyone tends to congregate down there on an almost daily basis. She has been one of the biggest inspirations in my life: she is gentle and selfless, she never complains about anything. My nanny is the most generous person I know and she genuinely cares more about us than she does about herself. She's hilarious, too. We will sit around for hours in her house just laughing. There is seldom a day I wouldn't make an effort to see Nanny.

As children, Peter and I went down to her house after school every day. We'd dump our schoolbags in the house and, as Mam and Dad were working, we would hop on our bikes and cycle down to Nanny's and we would get have our dinner with her. We grew up with her as part of our family and for a while she even lived with us. Everyone says my temperament is like hers, and I hope that's true – after all, I was named after her. Katie is of course short for Kathleen, and that's actually the name on my birth certificate.

While we were sitting in Nanny's house, we didn't realise that the celebration was still in full flight outside our home in Oldcourt. Nothing official had been organised up there, and I had intended spending the rest of the evening with Nanny. Then word filtered back that there were hundreds of people waiting outside our house to welcome me home. Dad decided to take a walk up to see what the situation was like. By this stage, we still hadn't actually been able to go home, because when we got off the plane, we went straight to the press conference and then on to Bray.

> Word filtered back that there were hundreds of people waiting outside our house to welcome me home.

Nanny Kathleen is such an important person in my life, and the lives of everyone in our family.

Trevor, my sister Sarah's fiancé, had been staying in the house while we were away and soon let us know it wasn't just a group but more like a thousand people outside and that they had been waiting there all day. One of the neighbours had rigged up loud speakers so I could say a few words, but Dad had to explain that I was exhausted because we'd been going all day. It was touching that so many had gathered there, as they had after I won the World Championship in China. That time we had brought the open-top bus into Oldcourt, where everyone waited to congratulate us. I stood for hours that day signing autographs for kids, and I'd loved it because they were all my neighbours. This time, however, it was about 11.30 and, sitting back in Nanny's house, I was shattered.

When Dad got close by, he was not sure if we would even be able to get into the house. There were crowds on the footpath, in the garden and even sitting on the car. I was genuinely taken-aback by

Despite the heavy rain, people still came to see Team Ireland as we paraded through Dublin.

their support and affection for me. Some had waited there for hours just to congratulate me. Dad promised them I'd come up in half an hour and say a few words, but that I was too tired to hang around for photos and autographs. How could we say no? After all, these were my neighbours who I grew up with, who I ran around the bank with as a little girl. They were a part of my story.

They were the people who had supported me from the start, from when I had had my first exhibition in the boxing hall to when I won my first World Championship. They were always loyal supporters and, when nobody else was interested in the teenage girl from Bray who dreamed of being a boxer, they were always there behind me. They had stayed out waiting to see the gold medal coming home and to be a part of something special for the area.

When we got home, I said a few words into the microphone – I can't now really remember what I said as I was so tired. The crowds gave me a huge reception and a big cheer, but when I had finished thanking them for their support they let me retreat to my house. Home at last. Everybody was still in festive form outside, so it took a while for things to die down, but eventually they dispersed and quietness descended on the house. For the first time in a long time, I was in my own home with my family. Within ten minutes, I was in bed and fast asleep.

> They had stayed out waiting to see the gold medal coming home and to be a part of something special for the area.

The Dublin Parade

We had been home from London for a few days when the idea of having another official celebration in Dublin's Mansion House first came up. The Olympic Council of Ireland came to us first, although I think the event was organised by the Dublin City Council. The idea was to showcase the

Olympic team and the medals we had won, but it was also a chance for me and the other athletes to say how much we appreciated the support the fans had shown and the hundreds of messages of encouragement they had sent throughout the entire three weeks of London 2012.

Unfortunately, the weather on the day was truly awful and that threw the plans into some confusion, with the organisers trying to implement some last-minute changes due to the rain. We started on a regular bus outside the National Stadium, where the elite Irish boxing team trains when they're in Dublin, and then headed to Farmleigh House in Phoenix Park. There we transferred to another bus, along with the rest of the Olympic team. The rain was pelting down, so there were few people around when we drove down the quays that ran parallel to the River Liffey. Despite the rain, several hundred people had still gathered on Dawson Street beside the Mansion House,

Taoiseach Enda Kenny welcoming me to the reception in Dublin.

where we would disembark to meet and greet some local politicians and dignitaries.

There were people cheering and waving from the cover of the shop-fronts that line the street. I was amazed that anyone braved the elements that day and I found myself wanting to stay outside with those that had waited for hours in the pouring rain to see the Olympic team. I wanted to go down and shake their hands and tell each one of them how much we appreciated their support in London and how much we appreciated them coming out on such an awful day just to get a glimpse of us – and that's all they got: a glimpse. But Irish fans are special, they are committed like no other. Some of the crowd would undoubtedly have spent lots of money getting across the Irish Sea to cheer us on.

I found it ironic that I was standing there with my fellow medal winners, cursing the rain, on what was meant to be a day of great celebration. Because, of course, I might have never set foot inside a boxing club if not for this same weather that was responsible for an athletics meeting being cancelled when I was nine years old. That night, my Dad took me to the boxing club instead. Who could have known that, all these years later, I would be standing under the same clouds, this time with a gold medal around my neck?

It was wonderful to see how the Olympics had brought everyone together, and what my medal meant to people – I have seen it bring grown men to tears! It not only symbolises my achievement, but it has come to represent the fact that barriers can be torn down and that dreams can be realised for ordinary people. After all, I am the youngest child of an ordinary family, who live in the middle house on a modest row of houses, in a council estate in a seaside town of Bray on the east coast of small island called Ireland. But I had a big dream. And an even bigger God.

I'd poured my whole boxing life into one week in London, and when I look back now, I know every second was worth it.

CHAPTER 9

SHAKING
THE WORLD

People have not seen the best of me yet.

Amateur or Professional?

At 26 years old, I'm still young and fresh. I look after myself, and my body is healthy. I don't drink or smoke, and lead a quiet social life. I pick up injuries like any other athlete; I have a back injury that can flare up, and have recently had a shoulder problem from overuse, but there are no serious fitness concerns. What's more, my mind is strong. I may have won my Olympic gold medal, but I feel I have some big years ahead of me.

The question on everyone's mind after London was: where will those years be spent, in the amateur or professional ring? The answer is that I will be spending the remaining years of my boxing career in the amateur ring.

I didn't always believe I would end up in the amateur ranks. Five years ago, I began to think of turning professional. With no guarantees of being able to compete in the Olympics, that seemed to be the natural direction that my career would take. But since then, the face of both the amateur and professional ranks has changed and so has my career path. Female boxers can now compete in the Olympic Games, which has brought about a surge in interest in the sport, while increasing frustration with the politics of professional match-making has resulted in a decline in interest in the professional game.

The best female boxers in the world are in the amateur game, so that is where I will stay. I intend to defend my European title next year and then go on to try to win my fifth world title in 2014 in Canada. After that, I aim to travel to Rio in four years' time and try to retain my Olympic title. Defending my titles won't be easy, but then I've always been ambitious.

After becoming Olympic champion, I had various offers on the table, so I went to Spain on a family holiday to think about what I wanted to do. The biggest question was what my next challenge was going to be. The decision was clear to me: I love amateur boxing and I love the idea of winning more major titles. They are all I have ever thought about and even if a tempting professional contract had come up, offering a life-changing sum of money, I don't know if I would have been happy making the move across.

Dad says that part of his job is to make sure I have financial security, long after I've hung up the gloves. You have to take this into consideration, of course, and I would take any big offer seriously. If Oscar De La Hoya came in with an offer of a $2 million signing-on fee next week, I would be stupid not to consider it. After all, boxing is a short career, and it could all end tomorrow with an injury.

When we were considering going professional, Dad spoke to several promoters and agents, including Irish boxing promoter and manager Brian Peters, as well as his contacts in the UK and the USA. Brian, who managed Bernard Dunne to a world title in Dublin, thought there might be an opening in the US. We also made contact with the former world champion and boxing legend Oscar De La Hoya. Some promoters said to Dad that turning professional was the only road left to take, because I was now 'at the top of Mount Everest' in the amateurs and there was nowhere to go from the top but down, apparently.

But I don't agree. To believe that the only progression from being an amateur champion is into the professional ranks is plain wrong,

> *I feel I can still improve, so that when the Rio Games come along I will be a better boxer.*

and to suggest that remaining amateur is some kind of resignation, or shows a lack of ambition, is nonsense. Defending my Olympic title in Rio in 2016 is going to be considerably harder than winning a world professional title. Remaining amateur is the more ambitious route as far as I can see.

I feel I can still improve over the next few years, so that when the Rio Games come along I will be a better boxer. Trust me: people have not seen the best of me yet.

People may object that I'm missing a great opportunity to earn money from the professional ranks, but I have been fortunate enough to make a good living from amateur boxing. Besides, the typical professional is only just making ends meet. Yes, the judging can occasionally be baffling in amateur boxing, but overall it is the purer of the two sports. I also believe that funded amateurs have a better quality of life. You are a member of an international team, which includes other boxers as well as coaches, physios and officials. But life as a professional can be isolated, and many new professionals struggle to cope with the transition.

My agents Pat Devlin and his son Mark Devlin at Jacqmar Sports.

Few understand that better than Tony Sutherland, whose son Darren won the middleweight bronze medal in Beijing, before turning professional. Darren was one of the most exciting professional prospects this country has ever seen, but he never got to fulfil his professional ambitions. Just over a year after his Olympic success, I was at the European Championships in Ukraine when I got news of Darren's tragic death. I was heart-broken, and wasn't sure if I was going to be able to box. Fortunately, I got a bye through the first round, which meant I had a few more days to process the grief and try to get my mind ready for the competition.

I met Tony during our homecoming after the Olympics. Like my mam, he had carried the Olympic torch on one of the relay legs through Dublin. His advice to Dad was that I should stay on as an amateur, as he believed that Darren had been unhappy as a professional. Without the right team around you, boxing can be a lonely sport, but especially when trying to climb up through the professional ladder.

The politics of arranging professional fights is another drawback. As an amateur, I never hand-pick an opponent to suit my style, I simply go to a tournament and take on whoever I am drawn to fight against.

Tony Sutherland, father of the late Darren Sutherland, was one of those who said I should remain an amateur boxer.

There is no plotting to find the 'right' opponent, or working out how I can line up a fight against someone who is trying to avoid me. You don't have to worry about how much clout you have behind you to get the big fight, or whether your promoter has enough sway to get you the fight you deserve. Who wants to sit around and wait for a fight to be agreed?

At the top international level, amateur boxing is harder than that: when I enter a competition such as the World Championships, I have to beat the best to be the best. There can only be one world champion.

Another source of inspiration, former world champion Bernard Dunne.

Earning that title might involve six fights in a week, all the while trying to make the 60 kilo weight. It is gruelling on the body and mind, and sometimes after a tournament my stomach has tightened up so much that I have to force food into it.

To be a world champion, I have to beat women who are the champions of their country or their continent. Two years ago in Barbados, I had to face girls from some of the most populous countries in the world – an Indian, a Brazilian, a Russian, an American and a Chinese girl – in five fights over six days. Each girl was a champion in her own right.

Professional belts seem to come easier than that. If you look at a large country like Great Britain, it has only ever had one amateur male world champion, Frankie Gavin, and one female world champion, Savannah Marshall. That's hard to believe from a country the size of Britain! In Ireland, we have never had a male reach a final at the World Championships, though we have had a few bronze medals – John Joe Nevin won two of them to become the first Irish male boxer to ever medal twice in the World Championships. Compare that to how many world champions Britain has had professionally. The figure could be in the hundreds, because there are so many different versions available at each weight under so many organisations.

It is true that many top amateurs have made successful transitions from the amateur to the professional ranks, and that the best professional male world champions have generally come from a good amateur pedigree, often winning Olympic medals early on: Floyd Mayweather won a bronze medal, Sugar Ray Leonard a gold and Muhammad Ali also won gold to name just a few. Indeed, Ireland's Wayne McCullough won a silver medal in Barcelona in 1992 and then went on to win a professional super bantamweight world title in Japan.

To be a world champion, I have to beat women who are the champions of their country or their continent. Professional belts seem to come easier than that.

But there is not the same tradition of crossover success for females. Very few professional women have come through the amateur code, and most have no background at all in boxing. They moved straight into fighting for money. Perhaps this culture will change with women's boxing now established as an Olympic sport. At the moment, it is hard to name a high-profile female professional boxer, with a few exceptions such as Holly Holm, who became the top welterweight after starting out in kick-boxing, then there's Muhammad Ali's daughter Laila and Joe Frazier's daughter Jacqui, but we only know them because of who their dads are. They never learned their craft in the amateur ring. Technically, the general standard at an international amateur tournament is far superior to the standard you will see on a professional bill, and any exceptions will be pro fighters who had good amateur careers.

So my heart is still in the amateur game and it's hard to see the bright lights of Las Vegas luring me away from the sport I love any time soon.

A New Career Away from Ireland?

There were a few other kites flown in the aftermath of the Olympics and the subject of football came up again, with some rumours floating around that I might be leaving boxing to go to London to play for Arsenal. I know my dad would have loved that, as there would be less stress for him if I retired from boxing!

Some of my friends and former Ireland team-mates such as Yvonne Tracy, Ciara Grant, Emma Byrne and Niamh Fahey all play for Arsenal. I had been thinking of dusting off my boots and playing

Lining up with the Ireland team, many of whom would go on to play for Arsenal, but rumours that I might join them there were just that.

occasionally for my old club-side Peamount, but Arsenal was never a realistic option. I'm not sure where that rumour started. Now, with time pressures and European titles to defend, I don't think I will be able to play even at local club level.

My decision to continue boxing means that Dad will be sticking around as my coach, though some of the other international boxing associations have tried to poach him away from me. He would never even consider it – imagine my Dad coaching other girls to try beat me! Not if they offered him a thousand times his salary. At one point, a very wealthy aspiring boxer, who was a member of the royal family of one of the big oil nations showed up at our boxing club to try to convince my dad to train him for the next Olympics. 'Name your price!' he said.

New Contracts and Sponsors

Bearing all that in mind, we are currently talking about a long-term contract from the Irish Sports Council, which would take me up to and beyond Rio 2016. It would mean that I can plan for the next four years. If I was unfortunate enough to be injured or had a dip in form while I was on a one-year contract, I'd come under pressure to keep the funding. A longer agreement therefore gives me some security. Even before women's boxing became an Olympic sport, the Sports Council funded me, while Dad has also been funded as a technical adviser.

Posing with Michael McKillop, Martin Cullen TD and Kenny Egan for an Irish Sports Council photograph – they are my most important sponsors.

It was good foresight from them to help keep us together as a team and we have built up trust between us over that time.

Of course there are other sponsors who support me, but the Sports Council is my biggest backer and I don't forget that. I know there is a good relationship between them and my dad, but it's not something I get involved in. I focus on my training and let Dad sort out everything else on the business side. Every Sunday we will sit down and work out what we need to do during the following week. Even when we're discussing working with a new sponsor, I won't go to any of the meetings. I know I can trust my family with everything.

Dad and my brother Peter will discuss the options and I know they will agree only to the best deals for me, the ones they believe are appropriate. They aren't always the deals that provide the most money, but the sponsor has to feel right for me. We have turned down some significant offers, because Dad understands who I am and what I think. For example, I wouldn't sponsor alcohol or bookmakers. Not because I think I'm better than someone who enjoys a drink or places a bet, but because those industries don't represent who I am. Sky are one of my sponsors, but we asked them to take Sky Betting out of my contract and they were happy to do so, because they know that is not what I am about. It is important to me that I don't sell myself for something that I don't believe in.

Of course there are other sponsors who support me, but the Sports Council is my biggest backer and I don't forget that.

Life Since the Olympics

There's no doubt that London 2012 has changed my life for the good, but there have also been superficial changes I've had to adjust to. People now know who I am and I'm more often recognised when I walk down the street. Simple things, like a visit to the cinema with friends, have become more complicated; and if I go out for a meal I am aware of people pointing and staring at me, or pointing their camera phones in my direction. It is taking me a while to get used to this, and it is something I find difficult to handle. I have no interest in fame or celebrity, and I have never made a decision motivated by trying to increase my public profile. I usually veer in the opposite direction. That said, I would give up my anonymity totally so long as I could keep my gold medal, but I want to live my life the way I have always done. And I will make every effort to do that.

There are the light-hearted sides to being recognised too. A few weeks ago, I was walking through a hotel foyer close to where I live on my way to a meeting. An elderly woman sitting by the reception looked up and recognised me, well kind of recognised me. She said: 'Ah it's Katie . . . Katie Price.' I smiled, said nothing and kept going.

When we sat down for the meeting, someone asked: 'Did I hear that woman right?' and we all burst out laughing. Dad said something about us being polar opposites.

The letters also started arriving shortly after I came back. The postman's stack for me was so big that he had to knock on our door because there were too many to fit through the letterbox. A lot of them were about my faith. I've had letters from mothers who told me they stopped what they were doing and went upstairs to pray for me on the day of the final. I received a beautiful letter from the president of the Methodist church in Ireland, as well as from Presbyterians, nuns, pastors, priests and people from north and south of the border, both catholic and protestant. I loved that people saw a faith in me that was non-denominational, and Christians from all types of churches were relating to how I was simply giving thanks to God for what He had done for me.

Often the envelopes don't even have an address on them, they simply say 'Katie Taylor champion', or 'Katie Taylor Bray', or 'Katie the boxer', or even 'Katie Taylor Best Boxer Ever'. I always open those first!

I've had letters from people from all walks of life and all ages. Little kids have sent me great poems that they've written themselves. One even sent a rap. It starts off: 'Katie Taylor you are not a failure . . .' Brilliant! Mam and I get a great laugh out of reading some of them, particularly the ones where I've received some odd requests for dates. I got one saying, 'All I want in life is health and you, Katie.' This guy then sent a letter to Mam and Dad to ask permission to take me out on a date. After that he sent me some photographs of him.

America and the President

One letter I took more seriously arrived through the letterbox just over two years ago. It was a formal invitation sent from the US Embassy in Dublin for me to go over to the States for a St Patrick's Day lunch in Washington and a chance to meet President Barack Obama. We stayed in this great hotel on Capitol Hill. It was the first time I'd been in America for St Patrick's Day, and Washington on 17 March is the place to be. There was shamrock everywhere and people were going around in their green ties and their green suits. When I arrived at the White House, I was shown to the Blue Room where we all gathered to listen to the formal speeches, including one from the Irish prime minister at the time, Brian Cowan.

Then President Obama moved around to meet people. When he came over to me, he said: 'So you're a boxer.' Then he took my hands to inspect them, to see if they were any different to anyone else's hands. I was nervous and honoured to be meeting the American president. I was humbled to have the opportunity to walk around the White House, not as a tourist but as an invited guest.

Shadow boxing with Michelle Obama.

I had the privilege to meet President Obama for a second time during his 2011 presidential trip to Ireland. I have a photograph of the president and his wife Michelle talking to me shortly after they arrived in Dublin. The first lady told me that her father, just like Dad, had also coached her to box. I remember her saying to me: 'If more women boxed in this world we would have a lot less problems!' I even managed to draw some shadow-boxing out of her – I was impressed by her stance!

I've been to the US a few times and had an interesting trip to Los Angeles earlier this year to shoot a commercial for one of my sponsors, Lucozade. They flew me out there first-class (the first time I'd ever experienced that luxury). I was taking part in it with the singer Tinie Tempah and drummer Travis Barker, and it was a very different experience for me. I didn't realise it was going to be such a huge production, and when I arrived on the set there were cameras and lights everywhere, and dozens of crew members running around getting things done. I'd never done anything like it – I even had my own trailer to rest in between shoots. I almost felt like a movie star!

I was on the set for three days, but we stayed there for a whole week so that we could take in LA. I didn't spend a whole lot of time on set with Tinie and Travis, except on the last day when we all had a scene together, but they were both so friendly and down-to-earth.

Dad and I managed to squeeze in a trip to the famous Wild Card Gym, run by Freddie Roach, and I took the opportunity to get in the ring and spar with the one of the Mexican fighters training there. When in Rome . . .

Irish promoter Brian Peters had called up Freddie before we travelled over to organise the spar for us. The gym was jam-packed with boxers and there was actually a queue to get in the ring. For me, the Wild Card was more exciting than shooting the ad. I was nervous and excited going there, because I had heard so much about it and

On the set of the Lucozade ad in Los Angeles with Tinie Tempah and Travis Barker.

> ## The life of a boxer is naturally more Wild Card gym than the Hollywood music set.

knew all the famous world champions, such as Manny Pacquiao, that had passed through. Freddie was there too. He was really quiet and unassuming. He doesn't get easily excited. He just kind of calmly looks around the place nodding, 'Good job, good work.' That was it – a man of few words.

What I didn't bargain for from the Wild Card experience was climbing out of the ring after my spar sporting a big a black eye. This was the day before the commercial shoot! When we went back to the studio they nearly had a collective stroke and it was panic stations all round. Fortunately, they were able to cover it up without any problem so you can't see it in the video.

We lived the glamorous life that week and stayed in the most amazing hotel, the Sunset Marquis in West Hollywood, just off the famous Sunset Boulevard. It is one of *the* places to stay when you are in Los Angeles. The first morning after we had arrived, we went down to have our breakfast. We were eating outside in this great hotel, the skies were blue and everything seemed perfect.

We looked across the terrace and Mam suddenly asked: 'Is that Gary Barlow?' And there he was, also having his breakfast. It turned out there was a recording studio in the basement of the hotel and anyone who is anyone in music has stayed there. Cheryl Cole was also there and so was Kanye West, while Stevie Wonder was in the hotel across the road.

But the life of a boxer is naturally more Wild Card gym than the Hollywood music set, and my best memories centre around the sport I love. The Hollywood glamour couldn't come close to my five European titles, four world titles and an Olympic gold. To top it off, I have recently been voted the world's best female boxer by the International Boxing Association (AIBA) for the third time. These awards come from sweat-shops like the Wild Card, so give me the grit any day.

Seeking the Five Rings

The road to women's boxing being included in the Games wasn't exactly plain sailing. But a defining moment in our campaign was in the 2007 men's World Championships in Chicago, where the president of the AIBA, Dr Ching-Kuo Wu, had asked me to take part in a demonstration tournament. Long before London 2012, women's boxing was lobbying to be included in the Olympic schedule and this women's tournament was to take place during the men's event as part of the process of convincing the International Olympic Committee (IOC) that women's boxing belonged in the Olympic Games. There were three female fights scheduled. I didn't realise how big my bout was until three days before it took place, when boxing officials called all the female boxers on the card in to a meeting. They said to us: 'Your performance will determine whether boxing is in the Olympics or not.' No pressure then!

It probably wasn't part of the official plan when I stopped my opponent in the first round of my fight. The crowd was going a bit crazy and wanted to see more than one round of boxing. I had given the IOC only a glimpse of what I could do, but they had obviously wanted to see more. After that demonstration, I was invited to another event to fight in Russia, and it ended up being like a World Championship, because they had invited the top ten girls in the world. Again, there were lots of officials from the IOC over to watch. I accepted because I desperately wanted women's boxing to become a part of the Olympics.

For a long time there had been rumours that women's boxing might be brought in for the Beijing Olympics in 2008, and even at a very late stage in the build-up to that event there was still an outside chance. In the end, my hopes were crushed, but in the early months of that Olympic year I was still training, clinging to some empty promises that it would be a last-minute inclusion in the schedule.

London 2012 did for women's boxing what nothing else could, and now it is established where it counts most: in the Olympic Games.

I genuinely believed that it would be included in the Olympics and was continually asking to find out if a decision had finally been made. My hopes were up because people kept promising things. Then, two months before Beijing, I was informed through a telephone call from a radio station that female boxing was not going to be a part of the Games. I was so devastated that I can't even remember my answer when I was asked on-air what I thought about the decision.

Because of what happened in 2008, I felt nervous ahead of London 2012. In the same way as previously, we were getting these promises from people that boxing would be included. The second time around, I was more guarded about setting my heart on it. But, as we now know, I need not have worried. London 2012 did for women's boxing what nothing else could, and now it is established and accepted where it counts most: in the Olympic Games.

I believed that if my sport was to flourish and to gain greater acceptance, we had to put our best foot forward and showcase our best talents. I always said that the best girls, even professionals, had to be able to compete in London. I thought this was important for its inclusion in 2016 and beyond.

I knew that huge numbers of people were going to be watching the tournament right across the globe and I said that women's boxing would shake the world. I pushed for the top boxers to be included, because I felt that if the gold medal was seen to have been easy to win, it would have devalued all of the other titles I have won in the World and European Championships. In a weak field, some would have rightly asked: 'Is this the standard of women's boxing?' With all the best girls in the ExCeL Arena, bar a few such as Turkey's Gulsum Tatar, people understand how competitive the sport has become.

Importantly, huge audiences will have watched the competition because of the blanket coverage on television. Prior to London, some people might have read about me winning gold, but few had ever seen me doing it. I won the recent World Championship this year in China, and before that I won my third world title in Barbados in 2010. My first two titles had been in New Delhi in 2006 and Ningbo, China in 2008. But despite my joy at these successes, it was frustrating sometimes. I was winning gold medal after gold medal, but people weren't able to see the boxing. Everyone just saw the results. They were pleased for me, but they had little idea of what was involved or how hard it was to achieve what I did.

The Olympics was a career first because it was the only time the Irish nation has been able to see all of my fights to win a title. I was overjoyed with the results of my performances, but I know I didn't

There were big celebrations in Oldcourt when I won my first world title in India, 2006.

In China after winning my second World Championship.

box my best in London. In other competitions, such as the European Championships in the Ukraine in 2009, when I was able to win the title without conceding a single point in the whole tournament, people would have seen the best of me. I will be working to make sure they will get that opportunity in the coming years.

My point is that it hasn't been easy to win my medals, and it is getting harder year by year. If I don't go into the ring against the likes of Sofya Ochigava, Mavzuna Chorieva or Natasha Jonas with the best conditioning and best tactics for those fights, I won't win. My rivals are trying to close in on me, and I'm working hard to keep one step ahead of everyone. That's how it has always been for me. Ochigava will keep trying to beat me, because she is a Russian and they don't give up. She is a great boxer and I know I am going to meet her again and again. That's a good thing and a good rivalry to have in the 60kg division.

In my category, there are perhaps a dozen strong fighters, and I am sure the Olympics will mean that there will be more coming through very soon. In China, Cheng Dong has been the top fighter for a long time, but she now has her own rivals there. In England, Jonas is unquestionably talented, but she has good competition from the likes of Chantelle Cameron and Amanda Coulson. In Russia, Ochigava may be the dominant one, but there are a lot of strong Russian girls biting at her heels.

Come 2016 and the Rio Olympics, I don't know what is going to happen or who is going to be on the way up. All I know is that I'll always try to be a step ahead. I still have things to prove. I feel I still haven't shown people the best I have and there is a lot left in me. Four more years. At 26, it seems like I'm starting over but I'm still young and I'm still fresh. And I still want to win.

Action from my exhibition bout in front of members of the IOC which helped bring women's boxing to the Olympics.

This is Psalm 18, and I always read this ahead of any bout as I find the words inspire me and bring me comfort:

1 I love you, O Lord, my strength.

2 The Lord is my rock, my fortress and my deliverer; my God is my rock, in whom I take refuge, He is my shield and the horn of my salvation, my stronghold.

3 I call to the Lord, who is worthy of praise, and I have been saved from my enemies.

4 The cords of death entangled me; the torrents of destruction overwhelmed me.

5 The cords of the grave coiled around me; the snares of death confronted me.

6 In my distress I called to the Lord; I cried to my God for help. From his temple he heard my voice; my cry came before him, into his ears.

7 The earth trembled and quaked, and the foundations of the mountains shook; they trembled because he was angry.

8 Smoke rose from his nostrils; consuming fire came from his mouth, burning coals blazed out of it.

9 He parted the heavens and came down; dark clouds were under his feet.

10 He mounted the cherubim and flew; he soared on the wings of the wind.

11 He made darkness his covering, his canopy around him—the dark rain clouds of the sky.

12 Out of the brightness of his presence clouds advanced, with hailstones and bolts of lightning.

13 The Lord thundered from heaven; the voice of the Most High resounded.

14 He shot his arrows and scattered the enemies, with great bolts of lightning he routed them.

15 The valleys of the sea were exposed and the foundations of the earth laid bare at your rebuke, O Lord, at the blast of breath from your nostrils.

16 He reached down from on high and took hold of me; he drew me out of deep waters.

17 He rescued me from my powerful enemy, from my foes, who were too strong for me.

18 They confronted me in the day of my disaster, but the Lord was my support.

19 He brought me out into a spacious place; he rescued me because he delighted in me.

20 The Lord has dealt with me according to my righteousness; according to the cleanness of my hands he has rewarded me.

21 For I have kept the ways of the Lord; I have not done evil by turning from my God.

22 All his laws are before me; I have not turned away from his decrees.

23 I have been blameless before him and have kept myself from sin.

24 The Lord has rewarded me according to my righteousness, according to the cleanness of my hands in his sight.

25 To the faithful you show yourself faithful, to the blameless you show yourself blameless,

26 to the pure you show yourself pure, but to the crooked you show yourself shrewd.

27 You save the humble but bring low those whose eyes are haughty.

28 You, O Lord, keep my lamp burning; my God turns my darkness into light.

29 With your help I can advance against a troop; with my God I can scale a wall.

30 As for God, his way is perfect: The word of the Lord is flawless. He is a shield for all who take refuge in him.

31 For who is God besides the Lord? And who is the Rock except our God?

32 It is God who arms me with strength and makes my way perfect.

33 He makes my feet like the feet of a deer; he enables me to stand on the heights.

34 He trains my hands for battle; my arms can bend a bow of bronze.

35 You give me your shield of victory, and your right hand sustains me; you stoop down to make me great.

36 You broaden the path beneath me, so that my ankles do not turn over.

37 I pursued my enemies and overtook them; I did not turn back till they were destroyed.

38 I crushed them so that they could not rise; they fell beneath my feet.

39 You armed me with strength for battle; you made my adversaries bow at my feet.

40 You made my enemies turn their backs in flight, and I destroyed my foes.

41 They cried for help, but there was no one to save them—to the Lord, but he did not answer.

42 I beat them as fine as dust borne on the wind; I poured them out like mud in the streets.

43 You have delivered me from the attacks of the people; you have made me the head of nations. People I did not know are subject to me.

44 As soon as they hear me, they obey me; foreigners cringe before me.

45 They all lose heart; they come trembling from their strongholds.

46 The Lord lives! Praise be to my Rock! Exalted be God my Saviour!

47 He is the God who avenges me, who subdues nations under me,

48 Who saves me from my enemies. You exalted me above my foes; from a violent man you rescued me.

49 Therefore I will praise you among the nations, O Lord; I will sing praises to your name.

50 He gives his king great victories; he shows unfailing love to his anointed, to David and to his descendants forever.

I dedicate this book to my nanny Kathleen.

Your generosity, strength and courage throughout
your own life has been an inspiration to me.

ACKNOWLEDGEMENTS

Firstly, I would like to thank God for giving me my Olympic dream as well as the ability to fulfil it. In Him, all things are possible.

A huge thank you to Johnny Watterson. You had the most difficult task of drawing blood from a stone, but you did it.

Thanks to Marianne Gunn O'Connor and everyone at Simon & Schuster who has worked tirelessly on this book, in particular Ian Marshall, Jacqui Caulton and Kyle McEnery. Thanks also to my brother Peter who helped with the editing and the Wilton Hotel, Bray for their hospitality.

I would like to thank my parents for laying down their lives for my dream, I love you both more than I could ever express in words.

To my entire family, thank you for being a tower of strength for me over the years, especially in the build-up to the Olympics.

My heartfelt thanks to all at St Mark's Church for all your prayers and encouragement.

I would like to thank Zauri Antia, nobody has impacted Irish boxing more than you. My thanks to Billy Walsh and the High Performance team, and to the Irish Amateur Boxing Association for your support, particularly over the last couple of years. Thanks also to all at Bray Boxing Club.

My thanks to the Irish Sports Council for their support and funding over the years, and to all my sponsors, it is a pleasure working with you.

Finally, to all who have gone unmentioned, every friend, every teacher, every coach, and every supporter who brought down the roof in the ExCeL, to every single person who prayed for me, you have all played an important part in my story, thank you.

PICTURE CREDITS